Marilyn Sharpe

W9-CMV-049

for
Heaven's
Sake!

Parenting Preschoolers Faithfully

To Leah,
As you begin this transforming
journey of being family
Love and blessings,

Quill House Publishers
Minneapolis

Marilyn Sharpe

For Heaven's Sake!
Parenting Preschoolers Faithfully

Cover images:
Woman and child, courtesy of Tom and Jodee Iten. Used by permission.
Smaller family images © istockphoto.com.

Publishing consultant: Huff Publishing Associates, LLC
Cover and book design: Hillspring Books, Inc.

ISBN 978-1-933794-25-9

Quill House Publishers
P.O. Box 390759
Minneapolis, MN 55439

Manufactured in the U.S.A.

Contents!

PART 2
Raising a Child Others Can Love

PART 3
Parenting through the Hard Times

This book is dedicated to

* * * * * * * * * * * * * * * *

my beloved husband, Les

our beloved children
Alison, Kathryn, and Jonathan

our beloved grandchildren
Hayden, Erica, and Bennett

* * * * * * * * * * * * * * *

This circle of love continues to expand . . .
for heaven's sake!

Prologue

THIS BOOK has been in a reluctant birthing process for more than two decades. My husband, Les, began encouraging, urging, and nudging me to write a book more than twenty years ago. I brushed that idea away, claiming that I talked my books! For more than thirty years, I have been a parent educator, teaching classes and running a weekly parents' group in my congregation. Participants occasionally suggested turning my class into a book. Then my colleagues and friends at Vibrant Faith Ministries thought the time had come. I felt ganged up on, in a loving way.

With the sense of having stood on the high dive too long, I took the plunge. Now I invite you along. We will get wet, splashed with the promise of baptism. We will claim Jesus' promise to be with us always. We will examine what it means to understand parenting as a quintessentially spiritual journey. We will be surrounded and held by the wisdom of the experts— those in the field of child development who daily live with and shape the lives of children—and by children themselves.

I owe an enormous debt of gratitude to my family—parents, husband, children and their beloveds, and grandchildren—who have been my grace-filled learning laboratory. They have loved me and forgiven the mistakes I have made along the way. They have lived that unconditional love for me, which makes me want to be a better person, to be all that God has created me to be. They have been the face and voice and hands of Jesus to me. God has blessed me with them.

Thirty years' worth of incredible parents have gathered every week to pour out their stories, struggles, triumphs, and lived wisdom with me and with one another. They have been vulnerable, loving, and supportive. They have been family, the body of Christ. They are the parents we would wish for every child. God has blessed me with them.

My other family is made up of my fabulous colleagues at Vibrant Faith Ministries. Individually and collectively, they have nurtured me in faith and friendship, stretched and supported me to grow, believed in me when I wasn't so sure, and invited me to journey with them in equipping families to become the center for nurturing a vibrant, life-transforming faith in Jesus Christ. God has blessed me with them.

To all of my wondrous friends, faith parents, and extended family, I owe a thousand thanks and all my gratitude. They have shaped me, and I wear their fingerprints all over my life. God has blessed me with them.

And to this God, who claimed me in the waters of my baptism, called me beloved and forgiven, named me a child of God— this book is yours, in thanksgiving.

Blessings,
Marilyn

Introduction

THERE IS A GLUT of parenting books on the market. Many give advice on how to raise children, featuring skills, values, and tips. There are others that focus on faith formation in children. So how is this book different?

This book assumes that you want your child to have a vibrant, life-transforming faith in Jesus Christ. It is grounded in an understanding that, as parents, it isn't enough to drive kids to the church building and let professionals, or those trained by church professionals, do the faith nurture. Faith formation is braided into the dailiness of life together, delivered with the very best parenting skills available, and grounded in unconditional love. It's our job to pass on faith.

NURTURING FAITH AT HOME

Parenting and faith nurture are not two separate pursuits; they are most effective when practiced together as an integrated whole. The writer of Deuteronomy said it this way: "Keep these words that I am commanding you today in your heart. Recite them to your children and talk about them when you are at home and when you are away, when you lie down and when you rise" (6:6-7).

Okay, so this means that faith talk is supposed to suffuse all of life together. But is it really that important?

Parents are vitally important in passing on faith to children and youth. Factors in whether or not our children will have faith include what mom does, what dad does, what mom says, and what dad says. But if only one family in ten that attends church has faith-filled conversations outside the congregational building,* how will we begin?

This book provides simple, everyday ways to nurture faith in the home by practicing the Four Keys for Nurturing Faith.** They are:

* ✳ caring conversations
* ✳ family devotions
* ✳ rituals and traditions
* ✳ family service

The first four chapters will describe each key and give you practical ways to weave faith nurture into your life together. The Four Keys will be woven through all subsequent chapters.

The fifth chapter introduces the concept of AAA Christians.*** These are the Christian disciples that all of our children need in their lives. They are *authentic*, *available*, and *affirming*. As a parent or faith parent, you are that AAA Christian, the one who develops a personal and trusted relationship with your child. The Four Keys for Nurturing Faith and the concept of AAA Christians are part of the Vibrant Faith Frame (see page 7).

---

* From Young Adolescents and Their Parents, a 1980 study by Peter Benson.

** Rev. Dr. David Anderson identified the Four Keys in his doctoral dissertation, expanding them in the book *Frogs without Legs Can't Hear*.

*** Rev. Dr. Paul Hill, Executive Director of The Youth & Family Institute, first formulated the concept of AAA Christians, Christian disciples who make disciples. For more about AAA Christians and the Four Keys, read *Frogs without Legs Can't Hear* by Hill and Rev. Dr. David Anderson.

SOME ASSUMPTIONS

You probably have already guessed that I am madly passionate about both families and faith nurture. I am a huge advocate of families as the classroom for teaching all that is most important, the crucible for refining the best in each of us, and a safe harbor from life's storms.

The foundational assumption of this book is that *parenting is inherently a profound and transforming spiritual journey for both parent and child.* Both parent and child are beloved children of God, loved and forgiven. Additional assumptions include:

* The sacred is woven into the fabric of the daily.

* Parents are the first face, voice, and hands of Jesus to their children. Children trust and love God because they have first experienced trust and love with their parents.

* In return, children enable adults to see and hear God, if they make time in their relationships with children to experience God's presence.

* No parent feels adequate or competent in this role or is even sure what it should look like. That is absolutely normal. Parents don't need to know all of the answers or feel comfortable embarking on this journey.

* Families come in all sizes, shapes, and descriptions.

* Good, healthy families go through difficult, painful, and sometimes terrifying times. So it is vitally important that they tell the truth, don't try to go it alone, and get the help they need, knowing that healing and reconciliation are God's gifts and that God is present in all of life.

* Faith is a living, breathing, changing thing. The spiritual journey and faith formation are lifelong. Faith will grow and be strengthened through your experiences with your children.

❋ Growing kids faithfully will take you a lifetime and always be in process, not always showing results on your schedule or coming with the assurance that there won't be problems.

❋ Growing kids faithfully does come with awe in receiving God's child (whether through birth, adoption, marriage, or foster care) and knowing that this child is entrusted to your care, to love and nurture all God created this child to be.

IDEAS FOR USING THIS BOOK

Read this book in any way you choose, but here are some suggestions to consider.

IF YOU ARE READING ALONE. Read a section and stop to reflect, wonder, plan, and apply it to your life. Make it your own. Annotate it. Push back on the elements with which you disagree. Try some of the ideas, just one at a time. It was never intended that you do them all or do them all at once. Name and claim the things that you are already doing well.

IF YOU ARE READING AS A CO-PARENT. Read this together. Discuss it. Share what you have experienced as a parent. Be open and vulnerable with one another. Like those who read it alone, try just one new thing at a time, catching yourselves already doing some things very well.

IF YOU ARE READING AS A FAMILY. Try at least one idea from the family activities at the end of each chapter. Reflect on how you might want to tailor the idea to your family. Evaluate how it went. Come up with other ideas and do them.

IF YOU ARE READING AS A SMALL GROUP OR CLASS. Read and discuss one chapter at a time. Share with one another your experiences of applying the ideas to your family. Ask for ideas.

THE VIBRANT FAITH FRAME

The foundation of this book is the Vibrant Faith Frame, the core theological framework of Vibrant Faith Ministries.

Six Circles of Relationships

These are the relationships in which the Holy Spirit moves to stir up faith.

CHILD. Children and youth are in the center, often experiencing faith-bearing relationships among their peers. When we nurture faithful children and youth, we send them out into their peer groups to "go . . . make disciples" (Matthew 28:19). But sometimes, it is these young disciples of Jesus who stir up faith in adults.

FAMILY. This is the circle that holds the child and is the primary locus of relationships that shape the child.

CONGREGATION. Ideally, the congregation equips the family to nurture vibrant faith at home and out into the community and larger world. Relationships in the congregation provide faith parents for all the children and youth. Those relationships also provide opportunities for all God's children to live out their faith.

COMMUNITY. Beyond the boundaries of congregations and families, robust and surprising disciples may appear in our communities.

CULTURE. It is easy to portray our culture as anti-Christian, but our culture is rife with opportunities to serve. In addition, many newer cultures in our midst offer different ways to practice faith. How do we connect with them and emerge enriched by the experience?

CREATION. The Creator is abundantly and obviously present in the creation. Often we are blessed to have wonderful disciples join us in our experience of the creation—whether a walk in the woods, family Bible camp, or standing under the stars together and marveling at what God has done.

Five Principles

These are the principles for nurturing vibrant faith.

- ✳ Faith is formed by the power of the Holy Spirit through personal, trusted relationships.
- ✳ The church is a living partnership between the ministry of the congregation and the ministry of the home.
- ✳ Where Christ is present in faith, the home is church, too.
- ✳ Faith is caught more than it is taught.
- ✳ If we want Christian children and youth, we must have Christian adults.

Four Keys

These are the faith practices that nurture faith everywhere, all of the time.

- ✳ Caring conversations
- ✳ Devotions
- ✳ Rituals and traditions
- ✳ Service

Three Characteristics

These are the characteristics of Christian disciples, the AAA Christians all of our children need in their lives.

- ✳ Authentic
- ✳ Available
- ✳ Affirming

Faith Reflection

USE THIS DEVOTION from Deuteronomy 6:4-9 to open your study of the book. It is where Vibrant Faith Ministries begins and gets its sense of call to pass on a vibrant, life-transforming faith in Jesus Christ.

Hear God's call to you as a parent. Deuteronomy 6:4-9 is a powerful text to anchor your intention to be about faith formation every day of your life together with your child.

Begin by lighting a candle, remembering that we gather around the one who said, "I am the light of the world" (John 8:12), the same one about whom the Gospel of John said, "The light shines in the darkness, and the darkness did not overcome it" (John 1:5). You are gathering around this Jesus, this light, who is at the center of your family.

Read Deuteronomy 6:4-9 aloud.

Hear, O Israel: The Lord is our God, the Lord alone. You shall love the Lord your God with all your heart, and with all your soul, and with all your might. Keep these words that I am commanding you today in your heart. Recite them to your children and talk about them when you are at home and when you are away, when you lie down and when you rise. Bind them as a sign on your hand, fix them as an emblem on your forehead, and write them on the doorposts of your house and on your gates.

Then read the passage in sections, interspersed with the commentary.

Hear, O Israel:
> *Hear, O (wherever-you-live): This God is everywhere, and, more importantly, wherever you are.*

The Lord is our God, the Lord alone.
> *There is just one. God is the one and only. This is a First Commandment issue. And this Lord is ours.*

You shall love the Lord your God with all your heart, and with all your soul, and with all your might.
> *Love God with everything you have: your mind, your heart, and your might, which the early Hebrews believed was "all your possessions."*

> *Hold nothing back. Let love infuse everything you are and everything you do.*

Keep these words that I am commanding you today in your heart.
> *As contemporary Christians, it is so easy for us to keep these words in our heart but not hear what comes next—our marching orders as parents and faith parents to God's children.*

Recite them to your children and talk about them when you are at home and when you are away, when you lie down and when you rise.
> *Well, thank heavens, we only have to talk about God when we are at home and when we are not at home, when we are lying down and not lying down! Oh, wait. That means conversation about God needs to be braided into all of life, wherever we are, whatever we are doing.*

Bind them as a sign on your hand,

Now I see what the writer of Deuteronomy meant. Look at your hands. These are the hands that touch your child with great love, that comfort, that correct, that lift your child up. These are the hands that will leave Jesus' fingerprints all over your child. Your child will know that God loves him or her, because your child first experienced love from you.

Fix them as an emblem on your forehead,

It's the smile with which you greet others, friends and strangers, wherever you are. This same face shines the love of Christ into the lives of your children and all God's children, of all ages.

And write them on the doorposts of your house and on your gates.

This invites you to open wide the doors of your home to welcome God's children inside, your children, their friends, and children of all ages. The front door of your congregation is often not attached to your church building; instead, it is the door to the homes of those in your congregation. When you invite people into your home, where they experience the love of Christ in your hospitality, they are much more likely to accept your invitation to join you with your church family, too.

Take a deep breath. Now, we begin our journey.

1

Caring Conversations

I have called you by name, you are mine. Isaiah 43:1

GEORGE WAS a precious and precocious five-year old, when his Sunday school teacher asked the class, "How do you know you are loved?"

Without skipping a beat, George responded, "By the sound of my name in your throat!"

This is what the writer of Isaiah announces for God. God calls us by name and claims us. So how can we show God's love and care for the children in our midst?

The whole point of parenting your child of God is to express unconditional love. Not, "I love you, when . . ." Just simply, "I love you." This is the love God rains down on us in Jesus. There are no conditions or no terms. We cannot earn or deserve it.

The apostle Paul reminds us that nothing can separate us from the love of God we know in Jesus Christ: "For I am convinced that neither death, nor life, nor angels, nor rulers, nor things present, nor things to come, nor powers, nor height, nor depth, nor anything else in all creation, will be able to separate us from the love of God in Christ Jesus our Lord" (Romans 8:38-39).

The greatest gift you can give children is to love them unconditionally. Why? When children know that they are loved and secure, they are able to use their life energy to care for and about others. When love is conditional, based on behavior and accomplishments, the price children pay is huge.

WHERE TO BEGIN

How do you begin to tackle this daunting task of parenting faithfully? Begin with caring conversations, where all relationships begin.

Think back to your childhood. With whom did you have caring conversations as a very young child? How did those conversations happen? Where were you?

Many of us remember being nestled in a parent's arms, held on a lap, or playing with a parent on the floor while having a caring conversation.

For those of us who did not experience this, we longed for it. We sought it elsewhere and resolved to provide this kind of experience for any child we would parent. Some of the most nurturing parents I have ever known have provided this sanctuary for their children, despite never knowing it first hand. What a miraculous transformation this is for the parent as well as for the child.

David Anderson, pastor, scholar, father, and colleague of mine, wrote his doctoral dissertation on Lutheran spirituality in the home, emphasizing the importance of what goes on in the home, not only in the congregation. It was Anderson who named the Four Keys for Nurturing Faith, identifying them in scripture, in research on faith formation, and in the experience of God's faithful people.

Caring conversations are the floor under close relationships and certainly the floor under family life. They are the way we know one another and are known to one another. Caring conversations are one powerful way we model and transmit Christian values and faith to the next generation. Caring conversations help children experience the love of God. They are about being present: listening deeply, respectfully, and with great care; speaking with love and gentleness; and being empathetic. Responding to the daily concerns, delights, and insights of our children gives us their trust and invites them to express God's love to others. This is how God's love is passed on.

> Begin that lifelong, loving conversation the first time you see your child.

Begin that lifelong, loving conversation the first time you see your child, whether your child arrives by birth or adoption. Call your child by name. Tell your child he or she is beloved. Thank God for him or her. Beam. Coo. Snuggle. Caress. Sing. Some of your caring conversation will use words—some won't.

Actually, the conversation may begin before birth. A grandmother in Portland, Oregon shared this story. The first time she saw her grandson was in the birthing room, and he was less than an hour old. As she stood staring down at this precious baby, her son, Matt, called across the room to her. That one-hour old baby turned instantly in the direction of his father's voice, a voice he had heard before he was born. "I have called you by name" indeed!

The rational among us claim that it doesn't matter what we say, because babies can't understand the words we use. What every baby understands is the loving connection created by the sounds parents make. Babies need to hear language to acquire it. From tone of voice, they hear love expressed. They are comforted and soothed. Jesus told his followers that the sheep hear his voice and they follow him (John 10:27). So, too, our children do with us.

But conversation is more than what we say. It is listening and caring.

BEING PRESENT

Being truly present is where it all begins. This is a vital part of God's gift to us in Jesus Christ. Jesus came as the Word made flesh, to be fully present. Jesus' last promise to his disciples, then and now, is "I am with you always" (Matthew 28:20). It is being made in the image of this ever-present God that we learn what our children need: our presence.

And that is a whole lot more difficult than it sounds. We hardly know how to be present, even to ourselves. We live in a culture of distraction. It is a challenge to be fully present when noise and visual images, people and machines, are all vying for our attention. Then, there is the cultural expectation of multi-tasking. We aren't expected to focus on just one thing. It doesn't seem productive enough.

Remember for a moment someone who wasn't fully present with you. How valued did you feel? How hard did you want to try to communicate with that person?

Most of us feel devalued, detached, and distanced from those who are not fully present with us. The result is not the close, loving, and bonded relationship we'd all like to have with our children.

Now remember a person who has taken time with you, given you undivided attention, and modeled what it is to be fully present. You probably felt valued, cared about, and loved. You know you mattered.

How can we do this for our children?

Being present means being utterly focused on just one person. Most of us cannot do this all day, every day, with each child in our family. But make sure that each child has the gift of your undivided attention for some period of time each day. Ask another adult to be with your other child or children. Carve out the time when you are in the car, walking the dog, or tucking your child into bed. Here is what being present involves.

Be fully attentive

* Turn off the television, radio, computer, and MP3 player. Stay off the phone.

* Go to a quiet place, without others present.

* Face your child and be on the same level. Crouch down or hold your child in your arms or on your lap.

* Look into that precious face. Look into your child's eyes.

* Turn off your mind to all of the other tasks you need to remember or accomplish. Just be there.

For a stretch of time

* Give your child the time he or she needs. Being told to hurry doesn't make anyone feel important or valued. Some children shut down when rushed.

* Spend unhurried time each day with your young child to listen, observe, and just be available. The message your unhurried presence delivers is, "You are important and I love you."

Repeatedly

* Let being present, fully attentive for a leisurely stretch of time, be a pattern in your relationship. Plan to have it happen over and over again.

Cherish the time

❋ Use words. Say, "I love our time together." Say it with your smile and with your body, as you lean into your child and snuggle. Let your child overhear you telling someone else how much you look forward to this time together.

LISTENING

Being present, you are ready to listen deeply to your child. It means that you are seeking to understand, not just being quiet, waiting for a chance to talk. Use your ears to hear and your eyes to observe the unspoken messages communicated by body language and tone of voice. Use your heart to intuit what your child is feeling and thinking.

Katie asked her three and one-half-year old Emmie, "How do you feel when I listen to you?" Emmie responded, "Good!"

"And," her mother continued, "how do you feel when I don't listen to you?" "Not good," was the immediate reply.

What a wonderful way of both checking in with a child and teaching the importance of being a good listener. Listening involves both listening to your child and also helping your child learn to listen to you when you have something important to say. Here are some ideas.

Respectful listening

❋ First, take a deep, slow breath to physically slow yourself down. Listening is not a task to check off your "to do" list; it is your way of demonstrating the deep love you have for your child.

❋ Listen carefully and attentively when your child speaks to you (or make an appointment to listen when you do have time).

✳ Ask clarifying questions. (Do you want to know . . . ? Are you concerned about . . . ?)

✳ Don't interrupt. Interruptions say that you're impatient or not interested and leap to assumptions about what your child might say.

✳ Give verbal acknowledgements. (Oh, I see.) They let your child know that you are listening.

✳ Lean toward your child.

✳ Use gentle, affectionate, and reassuring touch. All of God's children need to be touched, and this is how our children learn to distinguish appropriate touch from inappropriate touch.

✳ Listen for feelings as well as for issues or situations or information. Acknowledge the feelings. (You are really disappointed to have to share my time with the new baby, aren't you?) Help name the feelings. (You look really frustrated that the train won't stay on the track.) Accept the feelings even if you have to limit the behavior.

✳ Take your child's issue seriously. Help him or her name feelings, especially the hard ones. Let your child know that you understand and care about those feelings. This is a powerful way to teach empathy, by modeling it.

Getting your child's attention

✳ Use eye contact. Look at your child so your child looks at you. Gently cradle the child's face in your hands.

✳ Get close together. Be on your child's level or lift the child to yours. Don't talk from another room or from across the playground.

✳ Use loving touch to help your child focus on you. Touch a shoulder or cheek. Hold your child.

✳ Minimize distractions. Turn off the television or radio. Don't try to talk to your child and continue a conversation with someone else. Move noisy toys out of the way. If other children are around, take your child to a quiet place apart.

SPEAKING

You know from personal experience that speaking is about so much more than the words that are used. When you talk to your child, think about the impact of the following suggestions on your caring conversation.

✳ Take your child and the issue seriously. It is just as disappointing for a child to discover that favorite pants are in the laundry as it is for the parent to discover an important piece of paper isn't anywhere to be found.

✳ Don't bombard your child with questions, especially the ones to which he or she is unlikely to know the answer. (Why did you push that little boy? Why did you eat the cookie I told you not to eat?)

✳ Give your child in fantasy what you can't or won't give in reality. For the child who is wailing about not being able to go to the zoo in the rain, say something like this: "Oh, I wish we could go to the zoo, too, and stay for a week. Which animals would you like to visit? I wish the zookeeper would let you feed the bears and swim with the dolphins. What should we be sure to do before we go home?" It says to your child that you understand.

✳ Express your love. Say it. Sing it. Hug it. Smile it. Make a heart-shaped picture for your child. Say it again.

✳ Give hope. (I know how frustrating it is not to be able to pedal your bike, but really, really soon, your legs will reach and you will be able to do it.)

✳ Use your sense of humor, but not at your child's expense.

✳ Use a gentle voice and don't raise it. If you do, use the opportunity to model apologizing.

✳ Be respectful. Don't use sarcasm, name-calling, ridicule, or put-downs.

✳ Pick your issues and stick with one. Don't revisit old situations.

✳ Talk about positive, fun things, as well as talk about chores, tasks, mistakes, and corrections. You want your child to look forward to hearing what you have to say, not dreading it or tuning you out.

✳ Catch your child being good, doing well, and improving. Compliment the action.

✳ Engage your child in problem solving. (Sam went home because you wouldn't let him play with your toys. Now you are really lonely. What could you do differently next time? What do you want to do now?)

✳ Keep it short. Don't lecture or repeat the reason you've given dozens of times before.

✳ Teach your child about prayer, God's gift of presence, listening, and understanding. Remind your child that God always listens and then pray a short prayer of thanks.

✳ Ask what your child heard you say or what you are asking her or him to do (or not to do). This is a way for you to check that your child both heard and understood.

✳ Use "I messages." Here's the formula:

> *I feel*
>
> *When you*
>
> *Because*
>
> *I want you to*

Instead of saying, "You make me so mad when you dump out your toys all over the family room," which sounds like an accusation and makes your child defensive, try, "I feel frustrated when you dump toys all over the family room. I just cleaned it up for company. I want you to pick up your toys and play with them in your room until our friends come."

Asking good questions

Questions such as "How was your day?" or "What did you do today?" are difficult for children. And questions such as "Why did you do it?" or "What were you thinking?" are even more difficult. Young children don't know the answer to these questions, and this kind of question slams the door shut on further conversation, relationship building, or enjoying time together. What is a good way to ask questions?

SETTING AND CONTEXT. Consider where and when you ask questions. Do you have your child's undivided attention and does your child have yours? Do you have time to spend on a conversation? Have you turned off the distractions? Are others overhearing your conversation and likely to use what they hear to taunt your child? If this is a time of conflict, tension, or high drama, postpone the conversation until peace reigns.

Great conversations depend on deep, respectful listening. They can happen when you are snuggling on the couch or tucking your child into bed, when you are in the car alone together or out on a walk, or when your child is in the tub or playing with you on the floor.

Make a date with just one kid to do something your child wants to do with you. Then, do it. Tell your child how much that time together meant. Remember it together. Do it again. This is a time where the only goal is to know and love one another better.

THE QUESTIONS THEMSELVES. Avoid *closed* questions, the ones that can be answered with one word. They sound like: "Why can't you share your toys?" "Are you picking on your sister again?" "Did you clean your room?" They close down the conversation.

Better questions are *open* questions, the ones that begin a conversation. They are generous, interested, and engaged. They invite others into a relationship. They sound like: "What do you like about Ben as a friend?" "If you could do anything you want to today, what would you do?" "What is hard for you about sharing your toys?" "What makes you happy?"

When you inadvertently asked a closed question, you can follow up by saying, "Tell me more."

THE ART OF LISTENING. This is a conversation's most important ingredient. No one is a better conversationalist than the one who listens, really listens to you. Give undivided attention. Ask further questions and give evidence of understanding and interest. Nod, smile, and lean toward your child. Don't interrupt. Remember what has been said. Ask about it as a follow up.

In Genesis 3:9, after humankind had already broken the relationship with God by sinning, God restored the relationship by asking a question, "Where are you?" Can't we follow this divine example of building bridges to one another with a good question?

FOUR KEY Family Activities

Caring conversations

○ Listen to your child—the words, facial expressions, body language. What do you hear?

○ Send members of your family off to nap, sleep, preschool, daycare, work, and play, telling them how much you love them.

○ In the car, turn off the radio, CD player, or DVD player and listen to what everyone has to say. Talk to each other in a caring tone of voice.

○ Answer your child's real questions.

○ Wonder aloud with your child if you don't have an answer to the question.

○ Hold and comfort your child when he or she is discouraged.

2

Family Devotions

Remove the sandals from your feet, for the place on which you are standing is holy ground. Exodus 3:5

THE FIRST TIME someone places your child in your hands, whether in the delivery room, in an orphanage, or at the airport, know that you stand on holy ground. God is present in this holy moment. Thank God for the gift of your child. Invite God to be present with you on this journey. You will never, ever be the same. Remove your sandals; life will now be lived on holy ground.

In Exodus, Moses stood before the burning bush and heard God speak to him. Why? Because Moses slowed down, turned aside, and noticed. To those of us who live life at hyper speed, how often do we slow down, turn aside, and notice that we are on holy ground? How might you do that?

PRAY

From the moment you know a child is coming into your life—
by birth, adoption, foster care, or marriage—pray for the child.
Thank God for the child and pray for God's partnership with you
in raising the child God is entrusting to your care. If you are co-
parenting, pray for the child's other parent and for yourself. If you
are parenting alone, pray for yourself and the other loving adults
you will invite into your circle of family to love your child.

If you are giving birth to a child, pray aloud, sing songs of
faith, and read aloud scripture or children's Bible storybooks
while you are pregnant. Current research from Canada, China,
and the University of North Carolina concludes that prenatal
experience significantly influences human newborns' earliest
voice preferences. Your child will hear your voice and recognize
it after birth.

When you hold your child, pray aloud. Pray for your child and
for yourself. Pray for patience. When you've had a day like the
main character in Judith Viorst's book, *Alexander and the Terrible, Horrible, No Good, Very Bad Day*, pray for God's peace, for
forgiveness, and for a fresh start. Visit the bedside of your child,
and, gazing at the face of your sleeping child, fall in love all over
again.

As a child of God, God wants to hear from you, too. Remember the gift of God's grace, promised at your baptism, received
in Holy Communion, and offered fresh every day of your life. Step
into the shower each day and let it be a baptismal reminder that
God offers to wash you clean every day. Accept that gift.

And, yes, children give us opportunities to pray for them.
Pray for other children, too, the ones you can name whose needs
you know and the ones who have no one else to pray for them.
Allow your children to hear and see you praying from the heart.
Your children will follow your example.

Tamara is a prayer warrior. Her five-year old daughter Christine and two-year old son Charlie know that she talks to God

every morning. Not wanting to interrupt one morning, Christine asked, "Mama, are you talking to God or can you get my breakfast?" Now Christine talks to God! This is the power of modeling. Kids "catch" these spiritual practices from us.

Say a table grace at meals. Let your child lead the grace as soon as he or she is able or shows interest. The content of the prayer is less important than teaching children by experience that we can take everything to God in prayer, over and over again, many times a day.

How often do we slow down, turn aside, and notice that we are on holy ground?

Get a book of children's prayers. Pray them with your child. Teach them to your child. Memorized prayer is a wonderful resource. Many of us grew up praying, "Now I lay me down to sleep . . ." and the Lord's Prayer.

Then, help your child learn to pray from the heart about current concerns and today's thanksgivings. Actually, children learn this quite naturally and may well become our teachers, reminding us how to pray spontaneously.

READ CHILDREN'S BIBLES

Jesus came into the lives of people of all ages and experiences, and spoke to them in the ways they needed to hear the good news. We, too, need to provide the word of God to our children in ways they can understand, to link God's story to their story. How can you do that?

Provide children's Bibles that are age appropriate. Get them at the library, a continuous and free source for age-appropriate Bibles, storybooks, and Christian music. Give them as a gift. Find them at a garage sale or used bookstore. Many congregations now realize how vitally important it is to provide Bibles at a number of times in the lives of children and families. It is still the word of God if there are more pictures than words.

Your four-year old is not wearing the same jeans that he or she wore at 18 months. Why not? They don't fit! Just as your child needs you to update clothing, your child needs a children's Bible that fits each age and stage of development.

In the same way that it is important for children to see the adults they love and trust praying, it is important that they see you reading the Bible, wondering aloud how this is God's living word for you today. One insightful parent said it this way, "If this is God's living word, I'd better open and read it, not just dust it!"

SING

We know that when our children hear advertising jingles, they memorize the simple tune and words, even if they have no idea what is being sold. There are things so much more important for our children to know than the slogans that sell sodas, gelatin, or popular seasonal toys.

Songs of faith help teach God's story to our children. These songs build an internal library of stories of God's love and faithfulness. Make sure they hear and learn children's songs of faith, such as "Jesus Loves Me." Also, let them hear and learn the great hymns of faith. Hymns and songs of praise help them make a joyful and thankful noise to the Lord. Christian contemporary music is a fresh addition to music that is faith-bearing. Living with children, you also know they will make up their own. Can you imagine the smile on God's face?

For many of us, music engages the whole being with the message. St. Augustine said it this way, "When you sing, you pray twice."

TEACH WITH TOYS

For every new children's movie that comes out, there are toys and DVDs on the market to help children tell the story and remember the characters. Provide toys that help children learn and tell God's story.

Noah's ark and pairs of animals can help children celebrate the diversity of God's world. Children love to match the paired animals and learn their names and the sounds they make. Use this opportunity to tell the story of Noah, the rainbow, and God's loving protection.

Get out a manger set (not just during Advent) that is age appropriate and can be grasped by chubby fingers. Put it on the floor, under the tree, or in your play area. Get down on the floor and tell the story of each of the characters who played a role in the birth of Jesus.

What other toys and stuffed animals might you provide for your child to help teach that God's story is their story, too?

EXPERIENCE CREATION

Child development experts are concerned about how little time children spend outdoors in nature. It has been dubbed a "nature-deficit disorder" by Richard Louv in his book *Last Child in the Woods*. What is the price children pay for being indoors or only in domesticated outdoor settings? Some children are afraid of the woods. They don't know how to play outside. They don't know that food is grown or raised, or what it looks like before it is shrink-wrapped in the meat case or put in a box or can. They are cut off from the wonder and vastness of God's creation. They do not understand themselves as part of God's creation, either. And, perhaps their greatest loss is not to connect with the creator of this incredible creation.

How can you reverse this trend in your family? Get outside in all seasons, at all the different times of day. Let children name the differences and changes. You and your child can experience this gift of creation with all five senses. What can you touch, see, hear, smell, and taste?

Be quiet and listen to the sounds of God's world. Look and name plants and animals, inanimate and animate elements of God's creation. Look up and marvel at light and darkness and the vastness of the universe. Children are naturally filled with wonder; catch it from them. Thank God for this creation.

KEEP BEDTIME RITUALS

Most of us have a bedtime routine for a child: tooth brushing, when they grow teeth; a fresh diaper or trip to the toilet; and taking off daytime clothes and putting on pajamas. With so little extra effort, bedtime can be a devotional ritual. In addition to the other stories and books you read before bed, add a nightly Bible story from a children's Bible. Sing a favorite song of faith. Say a prayer, simply and from the heart. And, after your child is baptized, make the sign of the cross on that little, beloved forehead and say, "Jesus loves you and I do, too." What a gift it is to bless a child. What a peaceful way to go to sleep.

LOOK FOR GOD SIGHTINGS

The church word for God sightings is "epiphany." It's happened to God's children throughout every chapter of human history.

January 6 is the day the church celebrates Epiphany, commemorating the coming of the magi to Bethlehem to worship the infant Jesus. What an unlikely scenario—scholars from the East bringing gifts fit for a king. They followed a star and astrological predictions, were challenged by the jealous and unscrupulous King Herod, and when they arrived to find the son of a peasant couple, fell down to worship this unlikely king! Elderly Anna and Simeon, present in the temple when Joseph and Mary brought the infant Jesus to be dedicated, recognized through the Holy Spirit this baby as God's redemption and salvation. This is the story of the entire season of Epiphany—people in unlikely settings, times, and places see Jesus, and through a knowledge not their own, recognize Jesus as the Messiah, the Son of God, the Savior of the world.

Now, 2,000 years later, the Holy Spirit still works through unlikely people in improbable places to recognize Jesus in daily life. Where have you met this Jesus? Are you on the lookout? Often, it is our children who help us with these sightings of the holy in the midst of the mundane.

> The Holy Spirit still works through unlikely people in improbable places to recognize Jesus in daily life.

Trevor turned four in mid-August. Too excited to sleep, Trevor was up before the sun and woke his mom. She wrapped him in a quilt and they sat on the patio, waiting for the sunrise. When the sun crested the eastern horizon, Trevor gasped and turned to his mother. "Mom," he exclaimed, "how did Jesus know that orange is my best color?" A meteorologist could have explained to Trevor why the sky was orange, rather than pink, yellow, grey, or blue. But it would take four-year old Trevor to declare the intimate presence of Jesus in his life. Epiphany!

How can you help the children you love to see the holy in the ordinary? Ask them where they have seen the presence of God. Name the places you see God's presence. Go on a God walk together, looking for the daily miracles. Wrap your child in a quilt and stand in the dark, marveling at the moon, gazing at the stars, or watching a storm blow in.

We can uncover the epiphanies all around us. Then, we can create a culture of gratitude, and with the psalmist declare, "O give thanks to the Lord, for he is good; for his steadfast love endures forever" (Psalm 107:1).

FOUR KEY Family Activities

Family devotions

○ Before your child can speak, pray aloud with him or her—and pray for your child. Never stop doing this!

○ When your child has some language skills, invite him or her to pray. Cherish the child's simplicity, trust, and gratitude for everything.

○ At bedtime, say a prayer of thanks recounting all the things for which you are grateful.

○ At dinner, say or sing a simple table grace. Have a collection of table graces from which to choose.

○ Read a story from a children's Bible. Wonder aloud what this story has to do with the life of your child.

○ Send all the kids on a hunt to find evidence in unlikely places of the things for which we can thank God, such as dirty dishes, too much food in the fridge, mud on the floor, toys strewn around, or laundry piling up. Gather, share, and thank God.

○ Say thank you to one another for those countless daily gifts, such as a hug, help cleaning up toys, sharing with a friend or sibling.

○ Cradle your child's face in your hands and say, "I see the face of Jesus in you."

○ Make the sign of the cross on your child's forehead—at bedtime, in the morning, or when you leave for the day.

3

Rituals and Traditions

And when your children ask you, "What do you mean by this obser-
vance?" you shall say, 'It is the passover sacrifice to the Lord, for he
passed over the houses of the Israelites in Egypt, when he struck
down the Egyptians but spared our houses.'" And the people bowed
down and worshiped. Exodus 12:26-27

RITUALS AND TRADITIONS with preschoolers? In Exodus,
God invites us to practice God-bearing rituals and traditions
with our children. God does not make age a prerequisite to this
practice; we shouldn't either.

Before the birth of a child, all families already have a multi-
tude of rituals and traditions. How do you wake up one another,
say good-bye for the day, welcome one another home, and say
good night? How do you celebrate birthdays and Christmas and
Easter? What stories, recipes, activities, and values shape your
identity as a family? How do you pray for a family member who is
experiencing a difficult situation or dealing with stress?

When we find God in the midst of these daily or seasonal
experiences, we will suffuse family life with God's presence.
Then it is clear what a family values, believes, and promotes, and
how faith shapes us individually and as a family.

So, what are some rituals and traditions we can do with preschoolers?

WORSHIPING TOGETHER

It is vitally important to gather as a family, with a congregational faith family, to worship together. No, it isn't easy, when you begin bringing young children to worship. They wiggle. They make noise. They don't understand some of the words. They can't read.

But when do you start? I've heard parents say they'll bring them when they can understand the sermon or when they can sit still and behave. When would that be? If we wait until they have cognitive development to understand a sermon, they will be embarrassed not to know what happens during the service or how to participate.

So, begin when they are young. What children will understand is that they are with the people they love most, and that worship matters to these beloved adults.

So, what are some rituals and traditions we can do with preschoolers?

Long before they understand the words, children will learn prayers, the creed, and hymns. They will learn the rhythms of worship. They will learn the smiling faces of their faith family. They will know that they belong.

Sit up close, where children can see and be engaged in worship. Run your finger under the words in the bulletin or worship book. Cover their little hands with yours to pray. Sing the hymns during the week. Pray the Lord's Prayer at home. After worship or when the sanctuary is not in use, let them explore. Give them names for structures. Tell them the stories depicted in stained glass windows or paintings.

Remember, it was Jesus who welcomed the children, saying, "Let the little children come to me; do not stop them; for it is to such as these that the kingdom of God belongs" (Mark 10:14).

BEDTIME ROUTINE

Do a bedtime routine however and whenever it works for you. If your child drops off to sleep in the middle of play on the kitchen floor, for heaven's sake, don't wake him or her up and do a bedtime routine as a forced march. If your child is a crabby bear before bed, make this an efficient, not elaborate routine, and create a routine filled with faithful rituals at another time of day when your child is relaxed. If the formerly beloved routine isn't working, be smart and stop doing it. If it has become elaborate, time consuming, and leaves you gritting your teeth, simplify, simplify, simplify.

That said, there can be something quite snuggly and soothing about a bedtime routine for both parent and child. Here are some possible pieces. Don't try to do them all. Pick and choose what works for you and your child, for your time and energy constraints, and gives both parent and child joy.

The hour before it is time to sleep, lower the lights, sounds, and stimuli in the child's environment. Turn off screens. Speak in a soft voice. This is not the time for rambunctious play and stimulation.

Often a bedtime ritual includes a final feeding, a clean diaper, and a change into pajamas or a blanket sleeper. It may involve rocking or walking the child, murmuring loving last words before sleep, a prayer, and a blessing. Some of us sing a lullaby, a song of faith, a song we have loved since childhood, or one made up for this precious bundle in our arms. After the child is baptized, we may nightly make the sign of the cross on the child's forehead, reminding the child that he or she is loved by God. When they are a little older, we brush their teeth, read a book, tell a story, snuggle, rub that little back, and find the favorite sleeping toy, pacifier, and blanket.

Some children are temperamentally predisposed to fall asleep easily wherever they are. For some, going to sleep is a challenge. For most children, bedtime rituals are a gift. This is a signal to the child that it is time to sleep. It is a wonderful way to let go of the day and embrace the sleep that is to come. Children need to be taught to sleep. The bedtime ritual is a wonderful way to do that.

No matter how old your child, you can maintain a bedtime ritual. With much older children and youth, a bedtime ritual is an opportunity to reconnect at the end of the day, listen in the dark to what they may not tell you in the light, and to express your love one more time. Trust me, this is a treasure. Invest early.

SAYING GOOD-BYE

Whether the good-bye is a daily leave-taking at daycare or an occasional good-bye when a babysitter or grandparent arrives, parents have the chance to make this a ritual that is full of reassurance and love. With a child going through separation anxiety, it seems easier to slip out the door when the child is distracted, but it is an investment in a child's security to establish a ritual and promise to return.

What does your preschooler need to hear from you before you leave? Tell the child you love him or her. Say, "I'll be back. Know that I miss you, too. Have a wonderful time. God is with you."

If the child is currently having a hard time separating from you, encourage the caregiver to remind the child that you will be back. After the hug and reassurance from you, it is the perfect time for the caregiver to distract the child with a book, a toy, a song, or something else your child enjoys. Resist the temptation to stay until the child is no longer sad. This often extends tears. Leave matter-of-factly, with confidence and reassurance you may not actually feel in that moment. Your child learns that you are not distraught and that you will come back.

Lily was a toddler who cried when her mom left. Her mother kissed the palm of her hand and told Lily, "My kiss is right there, waiting for you, if you want it."

Sam was starting preschool and cried when his dad left. His father gave him a laminated wallet photo of the family to have in his pocket, any time he needed to see them.

It is perfectly normal for children to cycle through separation anxiety several times in their young lives. They learn to separate and it is an important life skill.

FAMILY DINNER

Family dinner may seem like an impossible dream with a baby or very young child. Keep your expectations realistic. Lighting a candle is our favorite family ritual. It reminds us that Christ, the light of the world, is present with us. Candlelight is soothing, even for young children. Three-year old Gabriel's parents offer him the ultimate incentive to remain at the table until others are done eating. If he stays seated, he gets to blow out the candle. It works for him.

Say a simple table prayer. A one sentence grace is perfect. When your child signals that he or she wants to pray it, don't worry if it doesn't include anything about the food. It can be a simple, childlike prayer of thanks to God for anything the child cherishes. Sometimes, the child's contribution is a resounding "Amen!" Some children love to hold hands for prayer.

Dinner also can be a wonderful time to share the events of the day and to name "God sightings" (see page 30) from the day. This may be the time your family does devotions, a simple way of marking God's presence in life.

Treasure family mealtime as holy ground with the expectation that the television is off so family members can be present with each other without being distracted. Even at an early age, set the stage.

SAYING "I'M SORRY"

The most important way to teach a child to apologize is to model it. It doesn't erode your child's respect for you to admit that you, too, are human and in need of our Savior, Jesus Christ. It is a perfect opportunity to remind your child that Jesus is always ready to forgive.

My least grace-filled moments were trying to force my child to apologize. If my child actually said, "I'm sorry," it usually came out as whining and insincere, not at all what I had in mind. A better choice for me was to tell the person my child offended that I was so sorry for what my child had said or done, and I was sure my child would be, too.

Public shaming didn't work either. Humiliating my child was a lose-lose proposition.

When the emotion had drained out of the situation, I talked to my child privately about what had gone wrong, predicting that soon the child would learn to change that behavior and to be able to say, "I am sorry." Our kids become what we tell them they are. Give them healthy messages, and remember how very young they are.

CELEBRATING BIRTHDAYS

It takes so little to make our rituals and traditions God-bearing.

Yes, you already know how to celebrate a birthday. But use birthdays to add the opportunity to say a prayer, thanking God for the birthday child and all she or he means to each of you. Another idea is to invite the children coming to a birthday party to bring gifts for children in need and donate them to a homeless shelter or to bring supplies for a crisis nursery.

For the next birthday in your family, give each person at the birthday meal a candle. Invite each person to name one thing to thank God for about the birthday kid (of any age); then insert the candle into the cake. Light the candles and sing "Happy Birthday" but change the final line to "May God bless you."

CHRISTMAS

What are your current traditions surrounding Christmas? When you have a child, it is a perfect opportunity to rethink your Christmas traditions, to make sure they reflect your values and carry the message you want your child to hear. Here are some of my favorite Christmas traditions.

> ❊ Have a chunky wooden nativity set on the floor. Lie on the floor with your child and play with the characters, telling the story. Then, let your child tell the story to you. If the baby Jesus ends up in a crib or toddler bed for a night, what a wonderful story to tuck in your heart and your memory bank.

> ❊ Serve a birthday cake for baby Jesus on Christmas. Sing "Happy Birthday to You" to Jesus. Watch delight spread over your child's face.

> ❊ With your child, buy a toy for a child who otherwise wouldn't receive one. Although it is so tempting to purchase one and donate it when you are shopping alone, don't. When children are two or older, let them select the toy (and don't buy them one, too). Tell them why you are giving it to another child who otherwise would have no gift. It is okay if they whine and beg. It's part of learning generosity in response to God's best gift to us.

> ❊ Invite two other families with young children to join you in visiting a nursing home or a person in your neighborhood who can't get out. Sing two very simple Christmas carols. These people will feel that Christmas has come to them in the presence of these children. After all, this is the season of the coming of a very special child.

> ❊ Have a number of children's books that tell the story of Christ's birth and read one each day. Leave them in the space you all share. Don't put them away after Christmas. This is the story that bears retelling all year long.

CHANGING RITUALS AND TRADITIONS

After years of visiting extended family for Christmas, you might want one of your new traditions to be celebrating Christmas in your home. Think this one through carefully. Make the decision early. Let people know what you are doing and why. Reassure everyone that they are loved and that you want to see them, and suggest another time for a visit. Sometimes, it works best to write a letter, and follow it up with a call, when the recipient has had a chance to think about it and begin to adjust.

No one likes to be surprised and many people resist change. Although your family may feel disappointed and hurt, it may come out as anger. Persist in responding with kindness, compassion, and understanding, but don't capitulate. You don't want to fight this battle over and over again. A note might say, "You know how much we love all of you and how much we have cherished our family traditions. Now it is time for my new family to create the same kinds of traditions you created for us when we were kids, to let our children experience the magic of Christmas in their own home, just as you did for us when we were children. We will all be disappointed not to be together on Christmas Eve and Christmas Day. We all have the week after Christmas Day off and would love to have you come to celebrate with us then."

FAMILY VACATIONS

Before you exclaim, "Family vacations? Who has time for that?" stop just one minute and think about what constitutes a family vacation. It might be an overnight at a water park, a weekend camping trip, a day at the park or the beach, a week at a cabin on a lake, a long weekend with grandparents, or a delicious Saturday at home with no tasks to accomplish.

What makes it a family vacation for you and your family? The only non-negotiable ingredient is the family! It is really important to include the entire family. This will be a time your family makes memories, stores up family stories, and decides who you are as a family. The location, the length, the events, the memories to be made, all these are yours to design to fit your family's stages, interests, time available, and budget.

This is the perfect opportunity to practice all Four Keys for passing on faith. (Most of them happen quite naturally on family vacations. This is just an invitation to be intentional about them.)

CARING CONVERSATIONS. These can start the minute you are in the car or otherwise on the way, even if packing wasn't a high, holy family moment.

FAMILY DEVOTIONS. Include grace before meals, thanking God for the gift of this time together. When you are awed by a landscape, a sunset, or the delight of new experiences, pause and thank God.

RITUALS AND TRADITIONS. Bless one another. Eat special foods. Everything you do together counts.

FAMILY SERVICE. Everyone pitches in with tasks. Pick up trash that isn't yours. Watch another family's child, to give a harried parent a few minutes of peace.

RETHINKING RITUALS AND TRADITIONS

All of us have rituals and traditions. What are your favorites? How can they become God-bearing, reminding us of the love of God we know in Jesus Christ?

Are there some traditions you no longer enjoy or that drain you of time and energy? Let them go. In our family, reusable gift bags replaced more time consuming wrapping paper and bows. Potlucks replaced elaborate dinner parties. Donations to favorite charities and causes replaced some gift exchanges. Time together in front of the tree, doing simple devotions, replaced a lot of running around.

Wish you had a new one? This is the truth. If you do something once and a child loves it, it is your new family tradition. Review the ideas in this chapter. Ask others what they do and treasure. Then, if it fits your family, give it a try.

MILESTONES AND BLESSINGS

A faith milestone is a marker along life's journey that says, "This is something important and God is here." It is time to pause, to celebrate, to share joys and sorrows, to give and receive support, and to reflect on where and how we have found God in our story. What a gift to your young child to frame all of life as lived in God's presence.

Milestones have their roots in our Old Testament history. Joshua hears God's call to lead the Israelites back into the promised land. When they arrive, safe and dry on the far bank of the Jordan River, God orders them to send a member of each tribe back into the Jordan and bring out a stone to add to a pile where they camp that night. Why? So that when the children ask in times to come, "What do these stones mean to you?" then their parents and faith parents will tell them the story of God's faithfulness and presence in their lives (Joshua 4:6-7).

God invites us to do the same today. Look around your home. What are some of the "stones" that help you tell the stories of God's presence in your lives? Is it the first ultrasound of your baby or the picture sent by the adoption agency to tell you about your child? Either could bring you to your knees, thanking God for the gift of your child. Is it a wedding picture of your grandparents, who passed on faith to your parents and, through them, to you and your children? Is it a cross, given to your child at baptism that helps you tell the story of that day? Is it a rock from the beach where you vacationed last summer and marveled at God's creation? Is it your wedding ring that helps you tell how thankful you are to God to have met your spouse and be raising a family together? All of these are wonderful "stones" that help you tell the story of faith to your child.

FAITH MILESTONES

Most of us grew up in households and congregations that did not name many faith milestones or mark them. We didn't see them all as markers on our faith journey. We can begin today, being deliberate about looking for opportunities to name and claim God's presence in the new, the changing times in our lives. And we can tell those stories to our children.

What are some faith milestones in the lives of families with preschool children? Some that we mark in congregations are baptism, baptism birthdays, receiving a first Bible, starting Sunday school, and learning to pray. Some milestones are most often marked in our homes, like birthdays, family gatherings, holidays, vacations, receiving a new pet, burying a pet, celebrating a pregnancy or birth or adoption, or grieving the anniversary of the death of a beloved friend or family member. All of these are opportunities to find God in our lives.

How do we mark milestones? We name them, give a blessing, learn about the milestone, and give a gift, as a tangible reminder of the milestone.

Perhaps the hardest milestone to mark with young children is the death of someone they love. Because adults are often emotionally overwhelmed and at a loss for words, we assume that children should be shielded from death. When possible, talk to children about death and the hope we have in eternal life because of Jesus' death and resurrection—long before they face the death of a close friend or family member.

The death of a pet, a baby bird, or a person they don't know well can provide an opportunity to begin the conversation. Many books are available to help parents talk to kids about death in age-appropriate ways. When someone they love dies, children need to be included in receiving information and participating in as much of the ritual as possible. Young children don't need all the details. Use simple language, but don't use euphemisms. (Telling a child that a grandparent is asleep will only make the child terrified of going to sleep.)

If children are excluded, they are often confused and frightened, feeling that it is their fault. Preschool children still engage in magical thinking, and a child may well believe that because he or she was angry at Grandma or misbehaved, Grandma died. Invite an adult your child knows and trusts to be present with (or for) your child, answer questions, or take a walk during the funeral. It may well be the young child who comforts grieving adults with a simple, childlike affirmation of faith.

BLESS THE CHILDREN

Some of the most profound rituals and traditions you will celebrate with your young child are blessings. At the National Cathedral in Washington, D.C., there is a beautiful cross that holds this blessing: Bless this child, O Lord, with your presence enfold this child in your arms of mercy, and keep this child safe forever. Amen.

So, what are blessings anyway? God is the author and giver of blessings, chief of which is God's unconditional love for each of God's children. God's blessing is conveyed in baptism, when God names and claims the child; splashes the child with promise; and gives the gifts of the Holy Spirit, faith, forgiveness of sins, and eternal life. As parents and caring adults, we can convey God's blessing with our words and actions. The sign of the cross on a child's forehead is a blessing. A prayer for God's loving presence and forgiveness is a blessing. A delighted smile that wreathes the face of a parent when the child comes into view is a blessing. A hug that says, "the fight is over and we are united in love" is a blessing. We can let each child of God know that he or she is God's beloved, all of the time, no matter what.

Jesus blessed the children, declaring them God's blessing to us. "People were bringing little children to him in order that he might touch them, and the disciples spoke sternly to them. But when Jesus saw this, he was indignant and said to them, 'Let the little children come to me; do not stop them; for it is to such as these that the kingdom of God belongs. Truly I tell you, whoever does not receive the kingdom of God as a little child will never enter it.' And he took them up in his arms, laid his hands on them, and blessed them" (Mark 10:13-16).

How will you begin? Begin when you can, maybe when you first know you are pregnant, when you begin to fill out all of the paperwork for an adoption, or when you know you will become a foster family or a blended family. Pray for the child. Thank God for the gift of the child in your life. Begin to collect children's Bibles or storybooks that will help you tell the story of God's love to the child.

When the child arrives, plan the baptism. From that day, or if your child is already baptized, begin celebrating the baptism birthday, the day God splashed your child with promise and claimed this beloved as God's own. Use the sign of the cross as a daily reminder of baptism with your child. Build and fill a faith chest with all of the mementos of faith: the baptismal candle, gown, certificate, cards, baby Bible, songs of faith, Bible story books. Keep filling it. Use it as a home altar or a faith treasure chest that helps you tell the story of faith for your child.

The last words of the Christian Old Testament point to the coming of Jesus, the Messiah. We will know the coming of the Christ, by these signs: "Lo, I will send you the prophet Elijah . . . He will turn the hearts of parents to their children and the hearts of children to their parents" (Malachi 4:5-6).

May God bless you and your family through all of your rituals and traditions.

45

FOUR KEY Family Activities

Rituals and traditions

○ Ask yourself, "What are the things we do over and over again as a family that we really cherish?" Make a list. Put them on the calendar.

○ Take informal photos to capture your family rituals and traditions. Look at how happy and relaxed you are. This is joy! This is your holy ground.

○ Brainstorm one thing you wish your family did—and then do it! Maybe it is a walk around the lake, the outdoor concert, fireworks, a picnic inside when it is snowing, dessert for breakfast on someone's birthday, the sign of the cross on a beloved forehead before bed or as the day begins.

○ Put out framed pictures of some favorite faith milestones— baptism, wedding, adoption of a child—as a reminder and conversation starter. "What were we doing in that picture?"

○ Count your blessings. Literally. Make a list. Let it be your prayer of thanksgiving. Share it with your family or create a family list. Post it where you will all see it and be reminded.

○ Begin each day or end each day or say good-bye with the words of the benediction: "The Lord bless you and keep you; the Lord make his face to shine upon you, and be gracious to you; the Lord lift up his countenance upon you, and give you peace" (Numbers 6:24-26).

○ Make the sign of the cross on your child's forehead at bedtime, when you are waking them, or when you leave for the day, saying, "Jesus loves you and so do I!"

4

Family Service

Then the righteous will answer him, "Lord, when was it that we saw you hungry and gave you food, or thirsty and gave you something to drink? And when was it that we saw you a stranger and welcomed you, or naked and gave you clothing? And when was it that we saw you sick or in prison and visited you?" And [Jesus] will answer them, "Truly I tell you, just as you did it to one of the least of these who are members of my family, you did it to me." Matthew 25:37-40

WHO SAYS service is important? God says. From creation, God has paired the privilege of enjoying what God has made with the responsibility to care for it, to be a steward. This responsibility is not about earning God's love; God's love is freely given. It is God's invitation for us to respond to the enormous love God already showers on us. Service is a "get to," not a "got to." No one is too young to begin living God's love for others. Doing service as a family is truly a privilege.

How will you share this with your preschool child? Begin with a children's Bible and read the stories of Jesus caring for others, healing them, and giving them what they needed. Notice that Jesus tells us to do likewise.

Perhaps most riveting is Jesus' parable of the good Samaritan in Luke 10:25-37. Jesus begins with the Great Commandment, "You shall love the Lord your God with all your heart, and with all your soul, and with all your strength, and with all your mind; and your neighbor as yourself" (v. 27).

When challenged to define "neighbor," Jesus chose an outsider, the outcast who showed mercy and served despite personal danger and cost. The Samaritan, who was looked down on by Jews, was the one who went to a Jewish man who had been beaten by robbers and left to die. A priest and a Levite, Jews in esteemed positions, had passed by the inert man, fearful that they would be the next victims. The Samaritan, "moved with pity," bound the wounds of the injured man, placed him on his own animal, and took him to an inn to care for him. When he left the inn, he paid the innkeeper to care for the Samaritan and vowed to return and pay anything else the care cost. That is what it looks like to love our neighbor.

It is an inborn drive to be part of the community we call family, to make a difference, to have a purpose, to be needed.

THE POWER OF MODELING SERVICE

Children watch everything you do. With young children, your actions speak louder than words. Never underestimate the power of parents modeling service. We all have daily opportunities to serve others. Courtney, a young mother, said, "Living with a four-year old is like living with a mirror that speaks to you. And, it gives you very honest feedback!"

Because "faith [and anything else worthwhile] is caught more than it is taught" (Principle 4 from the Vibrant Faith Frame), serving together as a family, linking the generations, is a loving response to what God has already done for you. Together you have a chance to talk about what you have done, why you have done it, and what you have learned. This is the way to make service a joyous opportunity to love God back, to say "thank you," and to be the light of Christ for others. Serving with children makes it a habit, a spiritual practice, a faithful way of life. And engaging our older generations, linking them to our children, is a way to share stories and build a sense of "this is the way our family does life—we serve!"

A word to those who co-parent with someone who does not share the Christian faith: This modeling isn't just for the benefit of children. Other adults will find service contagious and engaging (and perhaps less threatening than some of the other faith practices). Invite an adult you love join you in service, without need to preach about it!

A DESIRE TO SERVE IS IN EVERYONE

From the time they first begin to speak, young children implore, "Me do it!" or "I help." It is an inborn drive to be part of the community we call family, to make a difference, to have a purpose, to be needed.

It is often more work to let a child help with something that is easier to do by yourself. But then you may have to live with the result: the recalcitrant adolescent who never pitches in to help, who expects the world to wait on him or her, who has a raging sense of entitlement, and who is self-centered and self-absorbed.

So, let's start again. What can young children really do for service? How much can they really understand? Isn't it enough for just the adults to do it—or to write a check to a favorite charity? Why would you do service as a family?

Here's why. It is important for all children to learn what Marian Wright Edelman learned from her parents, passed on to her three sons, and advocated for all God's children in founding The Children's Defense Fund. As the daughter of a poor, black Southern Baptist pastor, she learned that, "Service is the rent we pay for living. It is the very purpose of life, not something you do in your spare time." In her book *The Measure of Our Success*, she says she and her husband measured their success as parents by assessing whether or not they had passed on to their sons a desire to serve all God's children.

For families, service, one of the Four Keys, is an invaluable opportunity to practice the other three: having caring conversations, naming God's presence through devotions, and having it become one of your new family traditions.

PARENTING IS FULL TIME SERVICE

That's true, isn't it? Parenting is service twenty-four hours a day, seven days a week. No breaks. No vacation. No sick leave. This includes all of us, those who are home full time, those who work outside the home full time, and everyone in between. Wherever we are, we carry thoughts and concern for our children with us.

Parenting is physically, emotionally, intellectually, and spiritually demanding. And, it is the most important work you will ever do. Author and psychotherapist, Virginia Satire called it "peoplemaking." God creates humankind and provides parents as stewards, helping children become all they have been created to be. No wonder this is such important and demanding work. It is vocation, God's call to us.

As a parent, you are not going to have to worry about how to fill your service bucket. Parenting fills it to overflowing. Let that overflow splash on the young children you love. Let them share the load and the sense of purpose.

So, do service and invite those cherished children to be involved.

HELPING YOUNG CHILDREN SEE THE NEED

A group from our church rings bells for the Salvation Army at an upscale grocery store every December. It has become a cherished tradition, as well as an opportunity to serve. As Saturday shoppers approach the entrance, hear the bell, and see the red apron, most adults avert their eyes, mumble something, and rush past. Not children. They are fascinated. They want to know what we are doing and where all the money goes. They want a chance to ring the bell and to put money in the kettle. I love talking to the children and to the parents who take time to tell their children about those in the community who don't have money to go to the grocery store or have a safe, warm place to sleep.

Pastor Linton Scott runs a one-on-one ministry to the profoundly economically disadvantaged in our community, connecting the surplus of some with the needs of others, through our congregation. Daily, members and non-members alike bring clothes, food, and all kinds of household items to his collection area. Nightly, he makes runs in his panel van to the inner city, where he feels God has called him to serve, matching the contributions to the needs. Beloved in our family for more than thirty years, Pastor Scott has helped our children be generous, not with what they no longer want, but with what they would want to receive. It has been a powerful lesson in generosity and stewardship for parents and children alike. They hear his stories, know where their gifts are going, and see those in need as children of God, brothers and sisters with whom we are called to share what we have.

How can you help your children see the need? Simply answer their questions. Narrate the world in which you find yourself. Talk about why the hungry and homeless stand on freeway off ramps with a sign or beg on a street corner. Share stories of children who raise money for a favorite charity with a lemonade stand. Use those rich teachable moments to discuss the needs in our world. Soon your child will astonish you with insights about those in need and ask to help.

CATCH THEM SERVING

Aaron, age three, was so proud to help his dad carry tools and put them in a box as his family got ready to move. Pausing to take a break, Ned ruffled his adoring son's hair and announced, "This is my best helper!" Aaron beamed.

One of my favorite pieces of wisdom that parents and their children have taught me over the years is that "our children become what we tell them they are." If we tell our children that they are serving, that they are helping others, they will grow up and become servant leaders. Unfortunately, the reverse is also true. If we tell them that they are self-absorbed and focused only on themselves, they will not disappoint us.

Children become what we tell them they are.

What extraordinary power we have in telling our kids who they are and then watching them become that. Children endow their parents with the ability to know everything. Then, they assume that all we tell them is true. Therefore, we need to be very, very careful how we use words.

So often, we think of "catching" children doing something wrong. What difference would it make if we "caught" them doing it right, such as serving? Let's thank them and tell them what a difference their service makes. Here are a few examples of opportunities to thank your children for serving within your family life at home.

❄ Your toddler brings you a diaper for the baby.

❄ Your child helps you clear the table or sort the silverware after it is clean.

❄ Your little one hugs you when you are sad.

❄ You are sick in bed and your child brings you a pillow and blanket.

❄ Minutes before company arrives, your children pitch in and help pick up toys and trash.

❄ While you are babysitting for a friend, the child you are watching cries and your child offers comfort and a favorite toy.

THE IMPACT OF NAMING SERVICE

Label what your child does and what you and your child do together, as service. Say, "Now that's what I call service!" Talk about the difference it makes. Help your child understand the difference he or she makes in the lives of others. Will it make your young child feel important? I hope so! God has already declared your child made in God's image. Your child is part of God's very good creation and is beloved, named, and claimed.

In my denomination's baptismal liturgy, the pastor lights the child's baptismal candle and using words from Matthew 5:16, charges the child to "let your light shine before others, so that they may see your good works and give glory to your Father in heaven." Service is a powerful way for the youngest, the oldest, and all of us in between to make Jesus' love incarnate again. This is powerful evangelism, in the gentlest, most loving of ways.

FOUR KEY Family Activities

Family service

○ Catch your child doing an act of service at home and thank your child, labeling it service.

○ Plan a family service opportunity and invite another family to join you in acts of service.

○ Read a Bible story about Jesus caring for and serving others.

○ Go on a walk at the park and pick up trash your family didn't drop. (Take along plastic bags for the trash, wet wipes, and baggies to cover little hands.) Talk about why we help take care of God's creation.

○ As a family, pack large baggies with individual packages of non-perishable foods. Keep several in the car, to give to people who stand on freeway off ramps or at busy intersections with signs that say they are hungry.

○ Welcome people when they come to worship, by serving as greeters, yes, the whole family!

○ At a time of natural disaster, invite children to select toys they want to donate to children who have lost all their toys. Adults can also select household items that others will need.

○ Around Thanksgiving, plan a family event to feed people at a soup kitchen. Use it as a chance to be thankful for all God has given you, including opportunities to share with others.

○ As a family, visit a friend, neighbor, or family member who doesn't have a chance to connect often with others. Bring cookies and lemonade and have a chat.

○ Be ready to be surprised, thrilled, humbled, and impressed by what your children will teach you in these moments!

5

AAA Christians

People were bringing little children to [Jesus] in order that he might touch them; and the disciples spoke sternly to them. But when Jesus saw this, he was indignant and said to them, "Let the little children come to me; do not stop them; for it is to such as these that the kingdom of God belongs. Truly I tell you, whoever does not receive the kingdom of God as a little child will never enter it." And he took them up in his arms, laid his hands on them, and blessed them. Mark 10:13-16

THE BIBLE IS FILLED with stories of AAA Christians. The mothers who brought their little children to Jesus to be blessed by him are wonderful examples. Against all social conventions and in the face of grumpy disciples who felt that the women and children were a bother, these mothers persisted. Jesus not only obliged by blessing the children, but declared that the children themselves were blessings to the adults.

WHAT ARE AAA CHRISTIANS?

AAA Christians have nothing to do with travel clubs or high-lighted maps. They are the adults who transform the lives of children by being present and passionately involved in their lives. Children meet them in all Six Circles of Relationships in which the Holy Spirit stirs up faith (child, family, congregation, community, culture, creation). They are the "personal trusted relationships" of Principle 1 from the Vibrant Faith Frame (see page 7). They pass on faith in Jesus Christ, not because they are seminary trained or work in a congregation, but because of how they live their lives, how they treat others, and how they share their faith. They consistently practice all Four Keys. They come in all shapes and sizes, all ages and walks of life, all venues and experiences. They are adults who exhibit these characteristics.

AUTHENTIC. Authentic adults are not perfect people. Quite the contrary, they are aware of their flaws and know they make mistakes. They tell their faith and life stories, and live their faith, even with those who are difficult to love. They talk about God's love and forgiveness, and model it for the children. Authentic Christians ask all the hard questions of God and recognize that faith is sometimes a mystery. They live the Four Keys and are Christians every day, not just Sunday.

- ✳ They have caring conversations and are great listeners.
- ✳ They do devotions regularly and look at the world through the lens of faith.
- ✳ They have rituals and traditions that are God-bearing.
- ✳ They try to serve and love others, and truly care about children.

AVAILABLE. Making children a priority, available adults are fully present in listening to and in caring for children. They pay attention. They remember. They take children seriously. They show up for the things that matter to kids. They don't bring an agenda to their time with kids, but rather listen to children, support them, and pray for and with them. They have time to give and show that they enjoy it!

AFFIRMING. Although they don't approve of every behavior, affirming adults see each child made in the image of God, beloved and forgiven. They carefully separate behavior, which can be changed, from personhood, which can't. They care enough to correct what the child does and to love who the child is. They expend energy and attention in noticing and naming the gifts of each child and helping the child develop those gifts. They catch children being good, and they compliment their efforts, as well as their achievements.

AN OLD TESTAMENT EXAMPLE
In the Old Testament book of 1 Samuel, Eli, the priest in the temple, was a AAA adult to the young boy Samuel, who had been entrusted to Eli's care.

In the middle of the night, little Samuel heard a voice calling him in the dark. Samuel woke Eli three times, thinking it was Eli's voice he had heard. Resisting impatience, Eli helped young Samuel understand that it was God who had called. Eli taught Samuel how to respond. "Speak, Lord, for your servant is listening" (1 Samuel 3:9). Samuel did as Eli instructed him. God spoke.

Eli was Samuel's needed AAA adult. Eli was authentic, sharing his faith and knowledge of God with the child. He was repeatedly available. And Eli affirmed Samuel's importance to the God who was calling and helped him learn to answer.

SPOTTED IN THE CHECKOUT LINE
During a Christmas shopping rush, I was in line to check out when I observed a father and a distraught three-year old boy. Close to the head of the line when his son melted down and dissolved in tears of frustration and exhaustion, this tender father pulled the cart out of line and lifted his son in his arms. Away from the crowd, he reassured his son that he loved him, would help him regain his control, and understood how sad and

frustrated he must be. I went to find the father to thank him, not only for the exemplary treatment of his son, but for being a role model for all of the rest of us. He was a AAA Christian and an extraordinary example of an excellent parent.

WHO IS THAT IN THE FAMILY PICTURE?

Five-year old Matthew drew a family picture in nursery school. When he brought it home in his school bag, his mom noticed something unusual: The picture of this family of five members had six figures. "Matthew, will you tell me who each person is?" asked his mom. Matthew named Mom, Dad, Brianna, Michael, and Matthew. "Who is this?" his mother asked about the remaining figure. "Oh, you know, Mom," Matthew replied, "That's the guy at church who is always happy to see me." Matthew is part of a faith family, with one extra AAA Christian!

AN IMPROBABLE SIGHTING

At a motel in the midwest, I met Elisha, who worked at the front desk and made an occasional foray into the breakfast area. As I was eating breakfast, two young brothers were selecting their food. Juggling a too-full glass of juice, the youngest one, a boy of four, lost his balance and the juice spilled. One look at the wide-eyed, startled, and concerned face of the child told me to act. "I'll get some help," I offered.

Through the doorway, we heard a voice call out, "I'm right here. This is no problem. I'll just clean it up." And in came Elisha, a warm, kind, caring young woman, with a smile and a towel. In one smooth movement, she cleaned up the juice and reassured a very concerned little boy. "Look," she announced, with twinkling eyes, "Now there's a clean spot on the floor!"

I thanked Elisha, for both her compassion and her cleaning. "Well," she said, "I had a lot of accidents and spills when I was young, and my dad was always kind." Now, Elisha is a AAA Christian, a living legacy of her AAA dad.

WHO WERE YOUR AAA CHRISTIANS?

Who helped you listen to God and receive the blessings of Jesus?

One mother of four reports that the Sunday school teacher she had at age three still sends cards and writes to her and her entire family three or four times a year. What a faithful lifeline and connection.

For me, there were many AAA Christians, beginning with my parents. They modeled the faith. We said grace before each meal. We prayed at bedtime. We worshiped together on Sunday. They made sure my brother and I were in Sunday school. They modeled justice, kindness, and walking humbly with God. They loved us generously. They made us feel beloved. They welcomed others into our home. They helped the neighbor. But my parents were born on the cusp of the Silent Generation, and they died in their 50s, much too young, without ever having told me in words what Jesus meant to them.

Not so my maternal grandmother, Agnes Carlson, who was God's own sweet gift in my life. She came to visit my parents for two weeks when my mother was pregnant with me, and stayed twenty-five years! Gramma couldn't tell a story of her childhood without Jesus as a main character. Nor could she read or tell us a Bible story without finding my brother Paul and me right in the midst. Prayer was her mother tongue, and we all knew that for her, it was a local call. She was utterly authentic, endlessly available, and indiscriminately affirming.

> AAA Christians model the faith. They are:
>
> Authentic
> Available
> Affirming

When I was growing up, my congregation supported my family to pass on faith. Miss Joy cared for all the babies and toddlers in a room that wouldn't pass nursery code today. It was a small room with hot radiators, furnished only with a rocking chair and Miss Joy's spiritual imagination and love for the children. She sang the songs of faith and told us Bible stories. And she loved us, long past the time we were too old to stay with her on a Sunday morning. She leaned across the divided door and stayed current on our lives and loves and asked about our walk with Jesus. There were countless Sunday school teachers, pastors, church staff, and choir directors who cared about us, encouraged us, and taught us about Jesus, as much with their lives as with their Bible stories.

Neighbors were there, too. Mrs. McLaughlin, who lived next door, shared her grown son's favorite children's books and warm greetings across the backyard fence. Patty Bratnober, mother of my brother's close friend, Johnny, made time to talk to me, take me seriously, model a full life as an artist and mother of four children, and be the woman I thought I'd like to be.

Never, ever is there too much love surrounding a child. The love of Christ is always passed on embodied in others. These AAA Christians not only bless the children, but they strengthen parents, too, as part of a sturdy network of resources for both generations.

WHO ARE AAA CHRISTIANS FOR YOUR CHILD?

Who are the adults that are AAA for your preschooler? How can you select, invite, and grow more AAA Christians for your child? They might appear in some of these categories:

* parents
* grandparents
* extended family
* godparents
* neighbors
* friends
* daycare providers
* nursery workers

* Sunday school or vacation Bible school teachers

* nursery school teachers

* health care professionals

* music teachers or sports coaches

* unlikely people who appear as God's own gift

Please tell the wonderful AAA Christians in your child's life how important they are and how much you appreciate them. Describe what they do that makes a difference and thank them. Name how important the relationship is in front of your child and the adult.

Be intentional about surrounding your child with these nutritious, transformational adults, who model a vibrant faith and pass it on to your little one.

RAISING GOOD GRANDPARENTS

When you find out that you are expecting a child by birth, adoption, foster care, or marriage to the child's parent, it is the perfect time to begin the conversation with grandparents-to-be about how you would like them to be involved in the life of your child. If you missed that opportunity, then start today.

Most importantly, this topic is best discussed as a dialogue between parents and grandparents. Ask the grandparents how they would like to be involved in the lives of their grandchild. Tell them how you would like them to be involved. You need both parents and grandparents to express their dreams, hopes, and concerns. Talk about spending time together—holidays and other times such as family dinners, casual visits, babysitting, soccer games, or swimming lessons. Are visits planned ahead and invited, or can they be impromptu and drop in? Will you vacation together, plan cross-generational trips, or do service projects together?

If there are two (or more) sets of grandparents, this will involve negotiations about "sharing" the grandchild. (And you thought it was hard to teach young children to share?) If both parents like and trust both sets of grandparents and if the grandparents like one another, harmony has a chance. If there is mistrust or there are different styles of relating to children, challenges surface.

Parents have the last word on establishing boundaries and expectations. If you keep an open and loving dialogue with the grandparents, the child benefits and gets to see adults modeling respect and harmony.

GETTING GRANDPARENTS ON BOARD. A gift you can give grandparents is to share how you choose to parent and why. By giving reasons for your approach to parenting, you invite grandparents to understand and be part of your team. Share your values; your preferences in activities, behavior, and gifts; and your philosophy of discipline. Ask their support for the way you have chosen to parent. Remember, some issues are simply a difference in style. It may not be a right or wrong, just different. It is not confusing to children to have things be different with different adults in different households. They learn whose rules govern where. However, issues of safety have serious consequences and require all adults who care for the child to comply with the same rules.

HELPING THEM BE SUCCESSFUL. Your child will be the winner if grandparents are successful. Help grandparents know their grandchildren's likes and dislikes, joys and fears, favorite books and toys, and sleep schedule and food preferences. This will help both generations enjoy their time together and build wonderful memories. Help grandparents understand the child's developmental stages. It is easier to know that a beloved child is dealing with developmental separation anxiety than to believe that the child doesn't like the grandparent. Bring along a favorite toy, nightlight, book, or blankie to help the child feel at home.

IF GRANDPARENTS AREN'T AROUND. When grandparents live far away and don't see your child very often, think about creative ways to bridge the miles. Talk about grandparents when you aren't together. Have pictures of grandparents at your child's eye level. Talk on the phone or over the internet. When you are together, take pictures of the child and grandparents and look at those pictures. Tell "do you remember" stories about shared experiences. Make extended family a priority.

What if grandparents live close by but are emotionally distant and aloof, choose not to have much interaction with your child, or are physically or emotionally unsafe for the child? Unfortunately, none of us can create perfect grandparents for our child. We do, however, have the responsibility for keeping our child safe. What do you say to your child? First, listen to their sad feelings about not having grandparents who are involved. Then, reassure the child that this is about the adult, not about the child. Let the child know that he or she is loved and loveable. Find neighbors, friends, or congregational surrogate grandparents and plan time together to build those relationships.

BUILDING COMMUNITY

God did not create us to exist in isolation. Jesus affirmed our close connection, calling us his brothers and sisters, which means we are family. The prayer he taught us begins with "Our Father." We need to claim our relationship to one another.

In order to surround our children with AAA Christians, we need to spend time as a family with others. Parents are spending more time with their children today, and that is a very good thing. However, they are spending less time with other adults and other families, and that is a not so good thing. Yes, plan time for family. Also, plan some time with others to build a sturdy community to which your child belongs and experiences other adults who are authentic, available, and affirming.

Consider your congregation as a faith family. Look for a congregation (or help your congregation become a place) that loves, welcomes, and values you and your child. It is an equipping place that is serious about vibrant faith formation for adults, offers support in parenting, helps you pass on a vibrant faith to your child, and offers your family opportunities to practice all Four Keys. It is family friendly and welcomes children in worship and affirms you for worshiping with your child. Others know your child by name and smile every time they see him or her. They celebrate the faith milestones in your family. And the congregation offers you opportunities as a family to worship, learn, and serve together.

Wrap your child's godparents or baptismal sponsors into family celebration of baptismal birthdays and everyday life. Friends, neighbors, and others who share your interests are all potential participants in your child's community. You need the support and companionship of other adults, too. We never outgrow our need for connection and belonging.

WHAT ABOUT ADULTS WHO AREN'T AAA?

Into every life come some adults who are inauthentic, unavailable, and not affirming. Sometimes they are downright mean and threaten the safety of our kids. What do parents do about those adults? If they are not relatives, close family friends, or next door neighbors, exclude them from your child's life. If you cannot avoid them altogether, limit exposure and always make sure the contact is short and supervised. Debrief the experience with your child after the visit. Be sanctuary for your child, offering a safe haven. Remember: You are the parent and you have the last word in who has access to your child!

YOUR TURN

Now, who needs you to be a AAA Christian? All God's children do. Not a single child or youth in your family, congregation, or community has one too many adults who are authentic, available, and affirming. No, it isn't possible for any one of us to nurture all of the children. Pick one outside the circle of your family who needs a AAA Christian. Practice being authentic, available, and affirming for this one child. This is your chance to pass on faith! Be prepared to be blessed in this relationship.

How do you act as a AAA Christian? Practice the Four Keys.

Caring conversations

❋ Answer their real questions.

❋ Wonder aloud with them, if you don't have an answer.

❋ Hold and comfort them when they are discouraged.

❋ Listen intently.

Devotions

❋ Read stories out of a children's Bible.

❋ Do devotions together.

❋ Pray with and for them.

❋ Remind them that God is present in all of life.

Rituals and traditions

❋ Tuck them into bed with a bedtime routine: a song of faith, Bible story, prayer, sign of the cross on the forehead.

❋ Say "good-bye," telling the children you miss them.

Service

❋ Invite them to pitch in and help you with a task; then thank them for their service.

❋ Catch them being helpful and say, "That's what I call service."

FOUR KEY Family Activities

- Ask your child, "What grown-up helps you feel Jesus' love?" Invite the children to tell a story about their AAA Christians. Make sure you let that adult know.

- Tell the story of a AAA Christian in your life. If that person is still alive, write, email, or call and thank them. Thank God for them.

- Catch others being AAA Christians and tell them how important they are.

- Which of the three characteristics of AAA Christians are you really good at and which one would you like to grow in and practice? Focus on doing that.

- Find one child who needs you to be that AAA Christian, then be it!

6

Knowing Your Child Uniquely

O Lord, you have searched me and known me. You know when I sit down and when I rise up; you discern my thoughts from far away. You search out my path and my lying down, and you are acquainted with all my ways. Psalm 139:1-3

GOD KNOWS each of us uniquely, then plants us in a family to experience this intimate experience. Ideally, family is the place you know and are known, love and are loved. But it doesn't happen automatically. To give this gift to your children, you need to be present and intentional.

WHAT DID YOU EXPECT?

So, you think you were surprised with the child you received? Imagine Mary's utter disbelief when the angel announced that she would bear God's son (Luke 1:34). And that certainly wasn't the last surprise that came with her son, Jesus.

Since our first child was born, I have experienced the Christmas story in many new ways. God's gift is so unbelievably astonishing. Why should I be surprised that God's gifts to me in my children would not also be surprising?

Before our first child was born, I did have expectations: a child who looked something like me, my spouse, or our relatives; a child who resembled us temperamentally; a child who shared the same interests and values. Oh, and I expected to love our child and to be endlessly patient.

Are you laughing yet? I did have a beautiful, healthy baby girl, for which I gave immediate and ongoing thanks. But, Alison was really big, and I thought all babies were small. She slept only six hours out of twenty-four, and I thought babies slept all the time. But I did discover a love that defied everything I thought I knew about the length or depth or breadth of love it is possible to feel for another person. Alison stretched my heart, and I thank God for that gift.

Children yearn to be known, just as they are.

It was clear from the very first day that Alison was her own person, and that did not change. She was strong, spirited, intense, inquisitive, and assertive. She knew who she was, what she wanted, and how she was going to deal with life. These have been fabulous traits as she grew up. They were just a surprise—and a challenge to parent.

One of her great gifts to us was shaping us as much as we shaped her. Her father and I are stronger, more open, and less smug because Alison molded us and showed us the way. She taught us that indeed God had knit her together in her mother's womb and that she was certainly "fearfully and wonderfully [and I would add 'uniquely'] made" (Psalm 139:14).

KNOWING

Children yearn to be known, just as they are. None of us wants to be compared to a sibling, cousin, classmate, or friend. Name your child's gifts. Each is uniquely created by God, with special gifts and passions, interests and fears, successes and challenges. Celebrate those differences.

How can you do that? Begin with careful observation.

TEMPERAMENT. Is your child an introvert or an extrovert? Does your child get energy from being alone or with one loved and trusted person, or does your child get refilled by being with others? Both personality types can grow to be very socially skilled, but be sensitive to what refills your child's energy and what drains it.

Is your child one with high energy or one who needs to be quiet and rest more often? Does your child see the world as primarily a place that is usually positive, safe, and welcoming? Or does your child see this world as a place that is negative, scarce, and threatening? These are issues of temperament, not a character flaw. It is just the way your unique child of God is. As loving parents, it is your task to learn about your child just as he or she was created to be.

GIFTS, SKILLS, PASSIONS, ABILITIES, AND INTERESTS. Over time, observe carefully until you can see the unique gifts of your child. Name them. Resist the temptation to assume that all of the children in one family will share interests, gifts, passions, or abilities. Don't let a child in your family believe that there is only one right way to be a child in your family. Sometimes we inadvertently give this message when we declare, "Juan and Maria, you are both such fine little athletes!" What if Maria is very coordinated and rides a two-wheel bike before Juan, who is two years older? Maria feels unappreciated. Juan feels pitied. Both know it isn't the truth, and neither feels uniquely known and loved by their parents. Name your child's unique gifts and talents. Celebrate the differences.

LISTEN. This is a caring conversation's most important ingredient. No one is a better conversationalist than the one who really listens. Give undivided attention. Ask further questions and give evidence of understanding and interest. Nod, smile, and lean toward your child. Don't interrupt. Do remember what has been said. Ask about it as a follow up. (For more ideas on good listening, review Chapter 1.)

ASK GOOD QUESTIONS. Questions can either close down a conversation or open your child's door. If you really want to know your child, questions are key. It is also vital to pair good questions with attentive listening. (Again, review Chapter 1.)

LOVE ONE ANOTHER
Jesus said, "I give you a new commandment, that you love one another. Just as I have loved you, you also should love one another" (John 13:34).

What would it mean to love one another as God in Jesus Christ has first loved us? Let's explore a few of the elements of loving our children with the love of Christ.

SEPARATE BEHAVIOR FROM PERSONHOOD. When you correct your child's behavior, make it clear that it is the behavior, not the person that you dislike. Say, "I love you Alex, but I don't like your behavior when you hit." This says to your child, "I may not approve of your behavior, but I always love you." We can change our behavior; we cannot change our personhood.

FORGIVE ONE ANOTHER. Before becoming a parent, I thought that I was patient, kind, loving, and generous. Then, I found myself yelling at a two-year-old whom I loved more than life itself. I dropped to my knees, held her hands, and said, "Can you forgive me for losing my temper? I am so deeply sorry." She did. Then and there, I knew what it was to experience the grace of God. Confession and absolution aren't just for Sunday morning.

LOVE ONE ANOTHER, NO MATTER WHAT. In Judith Viorst's book, *Alexander and the Terrible, Horrible, No Good, Very Bad Day*, we meet a little boy whose mother loves him, no matter how miserable and whiney he is. We all have days like that. Pass on that mother's love to your children.

LOVE THE CHILD ENOUGH TO CORRECT MISBEHAVIOR AND SAY "NO." Do it in a way that preserves the child's self-respect and affirms that you know your child can do what is right.

LOVE THE "OTHER-NESS." Love what is different about each person in your family. Affirm those differences in interests, gifts, and temperament as gifts from God to be celebrated, not fixed.

EXPRESS LOVE EVERY DAY. Express love in words, in loving acts of service, in little surprise gifts that delight, with physical affection, and by choosing to spend quality time together.

LEARN TO SAY, "I LOVE YOU." PERIOD. Not, "I love you when you are so helpful, get good grades, are kind to your siblings, or don't sass me." No, just "I love you."

This is what Jesus did. Can we do the same for family, community, nation, and world? Imagine what might happen if we, and our children, could pass on this love to all God's family.

CONNECTING WITH OTHER PARENTS

In addition to informal connections with other parents in your extended family, neighborhood, and circle of friends, join a parent education and support group. Look for one in which people tell the truth about life with children and name the messiness of being a family. Listen for people who are open about their frustrations, disappointments (with themselves, as well as their children), challenges, and sorrows. You also will hear from those same parents their deep appreciation, awe, wonder, and love for their children. You will discover wise and resourceful strategies for parenting. You will observe absolutely heroic parenting. And you will meet parents who have enough love and energy to support you on your journey.

EXPECTATIONS

So many of our expectations seem realistic to us. But are they? What about these examples?

* If I am a strong introvert, I expect that my child will be quiet, love to page through books alone, and be content to stay at home with me, while I read.

* If I am a high energy extrovert, I expect that my child will adore the company of other children and adults, and thrive in chaos, noise, and fun.

* If I love sports, I expect my child to throw balls and aspire to play a sport every season.

* If I am an artist, I expect my child to be attuned to the arts, both creating and appreciating them.

* If I was a good student, I expect my child to excel at school.

Unspoken assumptions can go on and on. But God stirs it up and we often get a child who complements and completes us, but certainly doesn't replicate us. Or, we get a child who is similar to us, and we are faced with our own weaknesses and insecurities, the very things we hoped not to see in our children. Parenting is always a process of figuring out how to live together and love the uniqueness in each person.

CHALLENGING SURPRISES

Edie had colic. Her mom Rachel was a nurse. Her dad Ted was endlessly patient. Both hit the wall after twenty-four hours of plaintive, inconsolable wailing from Edie. They cried, right along with their tiny daughter. They had tried everything they knew to do. They called the doctor's office and got good advice, but the crying didn't stop. They used their extended family network and their group of close friends for their best ideas. None of the ideas quieted Edie for long, but friends and family were a lifeline, providing simple meals and respite care so parents could take a walk, go to the grocery store, or visit a friend. Friends even offered a quiet place for her parents to sleep, while they watched little Edie. At three months, Edie's colic stopped and life became good for the three of them. Rachel and Ted were appreciative of their network of support, and, as soon as they caught up on sleep, they offered support to others.

> What would it mean to love one another as God in Jesus Christ has first loved us?

Bev had always wanted a baby. She was thrilled to be pregnant. After a textbook pregnancy, Ben was born. He was healthy, happy, beautiful, and everything she had ever dreamed of in a child. Then, the clouds of a deep postpartum depression rolled in and Bev no longer knew herself. Alan, her loving husband of five years, didn't recognize her. He was scared to see her so withdrawn and apparently disconnected from their baby. Tears, sleeplessness, fear, and terrifying thoughts crowded out the delight of having a baby. Her doctor was quick to diagnose postpartum depression and begin antidepressant medication and support for Bev, so that she was not alone with Ben. Bev's parents came and lived with them for three months until the darkness lifted and Bev was able to trust herself with Ben and finally experience the joy of being his mother. When Ben started school, Bev volunteered with other moms suffering this unexpected and frightening disease.

Neither of these families dealt with these challenges alone. Ask for and accept the help you need.

MORE SERIOUS, LONG-TERM CHALLENGES

Some parents immediately know that something is seriously wrong or outside the norm. A baby arrives with a significant birth defect. A baby has Down syndrome. A baby is seriously ill.

Or, after months of everything seeming to progress normally, something seems very wrong. A child who babbled or acquired some words is now silent. An active child stops moving, growing, or mastering the next developmental steps.

No parent should deal with this alone. This is the time to take the following steps.

* Get a good medical workup to get a diagnosis for you or your child.

* Ask your hospital, physician, or clinic to help you network with other parents who have dealt with the same issues.

* Find national organizations that offer information, support, and resources.

* Surround yourself with family and friends who are supportive.

* Say "yes" to all the offers of food, respite care, babysitting, prayers, a massage, or a weekend away.

* If your congregation is able to offer pastoral and practical support, say "Yes." If your congregation doesn't, let them know this is a significant need.

Jesus' last words to his followers then and now were, "And remember, I am with you always" (Matthew 28:20). Claim that promise and let Jesus' friends be present with you, too.

LOVING THE CHILD: HOW WILL I DO THAT?

Some parents didn't grow up in homes in which love and affection were routinely demonstrated and spoken. For some, there is a fear about how an expression of love will be received. Others think that expressing affection might embarrass the one speaking and the one hearing it. Some just assume that the other person already knows and actually saying or writing anything would be redundant. For others, there is a fear of "public displays of affection." So, why bother to change?

* Some people really don't know that they are loved or loveable. The assumption that others know how much they mean to us isn't always true.

* All of us need to receive the assurance that we are loved. Physical touch, as an expression of that care and affection, is crucial for physical and mental health.

* Look at the healthiest relationships. They are undergirded with love, respect, and affection that are expressed openly and frequently.

* Children who believe that they are loved and loveable tend to be kind and loving to others and to thrive in every way.

* Most importantly, we have this God who continues to declare love for us. Think of the Bible as God's love letters to us. God's supreme expression of love is Jesus Christ. "For God so loved the world that he gave his only Son, so that everyone who believes in him may not perish but may have eternal life" (John 3:16). God stopped at nothing, not even the death of Jesus on the cross, to express this love for us. Then, Jesus invites us to love God back in loving acts of service to one another, especially the hardest to love in our midst.

FOUR KEY Family Activities

- ○ Catch your child being good. Tell your child what specific behavior you appreciate. Be twice as vigilant to observe good behaviors and qualities as you are to catch them doing something wrong.

- ○ On a day when behavior has been challenging and difficult, wrap your arms around your child and say, "I love you." (This works for older children, teens, and adults, too!)

- ○ Catch your kids being kind, thoughtful, sharing, and caring. Say, "Now that's what I call God's kind of love!"

- ○ With a squirt bottle of syrup, write, "I love you" or make a heart on pancakes. Write the same message on a dessert with aerosol whipping cream.

- ○ For each child's birthday, write an annual love letter, expressing your love and describing the qualities you have most admired this year. Read it aloud and save it.

- ○ Say, "I love you," at every opportunity. You will never regret having said it once too often!

7

Teaching Values

Train children in the right way, and when old, they will not stray.
Proverbs 22:6

ALL OF US WANT to raise children with strong values, those principles that will guide their decisions and actions. How do we decide which values we want to pass on to our children? How do we teach them, training our children in the right way? And, really, when old, will they not stray?

You are always teaching values, but are they the ones you want your child to learn? This is your opportunity to be intentional and consistent. Parenting is incredibly hard work; it is living a life that consistently reflects what we say we believe.

When is the last time that you wrote down a list of your values? For many of us, this is an exercise we have never done, or certainly have not had time to do since the first child came into our lives. And there are so many values that are important. In order to make an impact on your young child, you need to choose just a few. For right now, choose no more than five.

Begin by making your list. If you are co-parenting, ask the other parent to brainstorm with you so that you are sure to include the values of greatest importance to both of you. If you are parenting alone, invite a trusted adult friend to brainstorm with you.

There are many more potential values than you will come up with in one sitting. That's okay. You can add to your list for the rest of your lifetime. My quick list yielded: generosity, empathy, faithfulness, gratitude, respect, honesty, loyalty, hospitality, flexibility, justice, integrity, responsibility, and humor.

Next, consider Jesus' eloquent statement of core values in what is often referred to as the Great Commandment: "You shall love the Lord your God with all your heart, and with all your soul, and with all your strength, and with all your mind; and your neighbor as yourself" (Luke 10:27).

Jesus gives us the plumb line to measure our values: Do they reflect:

- ✳ love for God?
- ✳ love for others?
- ✳ love for ourselves?

Which on your list of values are core to living the Great Commandment? Where do you want to begin with your child? Yes, it does mean that you will let go of some of those values on your list, until the others are firmly entrenched. It will be tempting to add a few, especially when your in-laws are coming for a visit! Resist the temptation. You will have a chance to get them all in. Raising children is a lengthy process and will offer you countless opportunities to cover them all.

AN EXAMPLE

I'll choose gratitude. I want my children to feel grateful and to express it. Gratitude is a way of loving and honoring all that God has done for us. It is a value that helps children appreciate what others do for them as well as understand that they can "love their neighbor" by sharing some of God's incredible abundance. Gratitude also invites children to see, celebrate, and be thankful for all they have been given.

We have an entire season set aside for gratitude: Thanksgiving. Hymns and prayers in worship give thanks for all God's bounty. Cards arrive, echoing thanks for this season, this opportunity to be mindful and thankful. Even fundraisers thank you in advance for your gift. As families and friends gather around a festive meal, many express their thankfulness for the food, for family and friends, for health, for good work to do, and for the freedoms we enjoy.

> You are always teaching values, but are they the ones you want your child to learn?

But sometimes with our children, we bemoan the lack of gratitude and are concerned about the sense of entitlement among children of all ages. As parents, we don't always hear a "thank you" for a ride given or a friend invited over to play, much less for the daily tasks of supporting the family. Gratitude is an opportunity to pause—to look, really look at our lives and say "thank you" to a God whose signature is abundance.

So often adults and children alike recount a litany of scarcity. We want more possessions, different relationships, skills we haven't acquired, travel we haven't done, a job or school that suits us better, recognition for who we are and what we have accomplished, and time. Oh, would we like more time! Looking at life through the lens of scarcity makes us dissatisfied and miserably unaware of all of the good things in our lives.

But God has showered us with abundance. All we have to do is open our eyes, our minds, and our hearts to it. Satisfaction, delight, and gratitude are ours, if only we pause in the headlong rush for "more" and celebrate "enough." How might we begin?

* Instead of a wish list, create a family thankfulness list.

* Celebrate the differences within your family. Give each family member a meal when everyone else says a prayer of thanks for the unique gifts of that person, expressing gratitude for all that person means to them individually and to the family as a whole.

* Set aside some Christmas money to share with a person, organization, or cause about which your family is passionate.

* Plan to share the holidays with those who don't have others with whom to celebrate.

* Find warm winter clothes that your family can give to others who don't have adequate cold weather clothing.

* Walk or drive around your community, pointing out the gifts that recent immigrants bring to your community. Tell stories about grandparents or great grandparents who were immigrants.

* Attend a cultural event of a culture that is new to you.

* Remember the elders in your family, congregation, or community. Visit them and learn from their stories.

TEACHING VALUES

How can we raise grateful children—or how do we teach this value? Here are seven strategies to teach any value.

NAME IT. Our children need to hear us say our values aloud. Describe them. Give an example of the value in action. Memorable examples often become favorite family stories that embody the value. In our family, it happened at a fast food restaurant after church. The need was the hunger of a homeless man, huddled over a bottomless cup of coffee on a frigid January day. After we sat down with our food, my husband jumped up and went back to the food counter to purchase a tray of food for the man. My husband's response to gratitude for all God has given us has always been generosity to those in need. This action was the beginning of many conversations with our children, who have all found their own ways to meet the needs they see.

MODEL IT. The most important lessons happen as we model the value, quality, trait, or behavior we want our children to learn. If there is dissonance between what we say and what we do, our children will believe and emulate what we do. If you want grateful kids, be a grateful adult.

Let them see and hear you saying "thank you" to those who wait on you in the shoe store and bakery, those who carry out your groceries, and those who change the oil in your car. Yes, you are paying for those services, but money never replaces gratitude. That is a human being who is serving you, not a machine. All need the dignity and respect of a "thank you." Your children are watching and listening.

If you co-parent, when the child's other parent does something that contributes to life together, say "thank you." When your child does something helpful, cooperative, or kind, say "thank you."

TEACH IT. None of our children is born knowing how to share, how to pitch in and help, or what we mean when we say, "Be nice." We need to model it, but we also need to say in words what we expect or what we would like. Gratitude is no different. Do a dress rehearsal before a child's birthday party or Christmas. Help your child practice saying "thank you" when anyone does something kind or helpful.

But please don't embarrass them with the patronizing reminder in front of the gift or cookie giver. "Now what do we say, Jamie?" Give them time to respond. And if they forget, model it for them by thanking the giver for both of you.

CATCH IT. When your child says "thank you" and expresses gratitude, make sure you point that out to him or her. Describe exactly what was said that you appreciate.

In parenting, one of my favorite lines is "what gets attention, gets repeated." It is true, whether the behavior is positive or negative and whether the attention is positive or negative. Since the goal of virtually all behavior is to get attention, it is vitally important to give positive attention for positive behavior, so that it will be repeated. (It is also important to note that negative behavior that elicits negative attention will cause that behavior to be repeated. So it is better to learn to focus on the positive.)

REMEMBER A TIME. When your child hasn't been grateful, remind your child of a time when he or she was grateful. Assure your child that soon he or she will remember to be consistently grateful.

DO IT OVER. When your child says something ungrateful or says nothing, invite him or her to "do it over." For example, your child can say, "I am sorry about what I said. I want you to know that I really appreciate the present you gave me." Never let children believe that they are stuck with something they said or did—or didn't say or do. Invite them to try it again, the way they wish they'd done it the first time.

PRAY IT. Daily, at the table, at the bedside, thank God for all of God's gifts. Remember with gratitude, the giver of all good gifts. Prayer is also a wonderful opportunity to ask for God's forgiveness and help when we haven't lived a value.

FOUR KEY Family Activities

- As a family, brainstorm your family values. Write them down. Post them where you see them every day.

- Catch people in your family living your values. Point it out. Name it as an example of your values.

- Have photos around that show your family living its values. Use them to retell the stories of those experiences and why they matter.

- Use a teachable moment—television show, movie, news, observing behavior of others—to point out examples of your values that are not demonstrated and discuss the consequences.

- Say "thank you" for the little things of daily life—holding the door, setting the table, sharing a toy, pitching in to clean up the family room.

- Let children overhear you being grateful.

- Make a list of things for which you are grateful and review it during family devotions, while sharing your day, or when tucking a child in bed.

- Take an opportunity to pause, look at your life, and say "thank you" to a God whose signature is abundance.

8

Helping Kids Figure It Out

"Choose this day whom you will serve . . . but as for me and my household, we will serve the Lord." Joshua 24:15

YOUNG CHILDREN often feel powerless. Adults determine what and when they will eat, with whom they will play, whether they will wear a jacket, and when they will go to bed. As a reaction to this frustration of having no power over their lives, children sometimes act out and have tantrums.

How can you give young children appropriate power and teach them life skills? Give them opportunities to make choices, beginning as preschoolers. When the child is young, the choices and decisions will be framed by parents. Parents will help young children evaluate the consequences of their choices and learn from those experiences. As children grow in age and experience, they will determine many of the choices and make decisions on their own, without consulting parents. The gift of early choosing, problem solving, and recovering from mistakes, will be that the child has learned a process and can predict the outcome.

CHOICES, CHOICES, CHOICES

The prescription for learning to choose is to make choices. Parents define which choices the child can make, what the two or three choices will be, and boundaries that limit the choices. Here are some examples.

 ❋ Do you want to wear your jeans or your red pants today?

 ❋ Would you like oatmeal or corn flakes for breakfast?

 ❋ Which do you want to do first, brush your teeth or use the potty?

Notice that the child was not asked what he or she wanted to wear. Many of us have discovered the hard way that when the child is asked what to wear to preschool, a tutu emerges in the midst of a blizzard. No, give two choices of clothing, both appropriate for the weather and the occasion.

Breakfast? The choices do not include steak or chocolate chip cookies. They include two options that are both available and agreeable to the parent.

Observe that the child was not asked whether or not he or she wanted to brush teeth or use the potty. The choice was in which order the child would like to do them.

So what if the child in your family responds, "No. I don't want either! Keeping your voice calm, smile and say, "Then, you are choosing to let me choose, and I choose . . ." Then you need to exercise the option you chose, even if your child then declares the other choice. Otherwise, you will confront this each and every time you give choices.

This strategy does not come with a warranty that your child will be delighted or always make a choice or even be agreeable to the thought you put into it. It does come with the assurance that your child has been given opportunities to make choices. That is what you have control over in this situation.

Don't give them non-choices, masquerading as choices: "Are you coming, or shall I leave you at the grocery store?" "Do you want to get into bed, or do you want a spanking?" Be respectful and clear about the real consequences: "You may walk with me now, or I will pick you up and carry you." "Get into bed now or there won't be time to read a story." Don't threaten your child with something you won't or shouldn't do.

CHOICES ABOUT HOW TO RESPOND

Parents need to teach their children that they have a choice about how they respond to their feelings. Teach them that they have every right to feel their feelings, but that they have choices about how they respond and behave. All children feel angry when another child butts in line for the slide. The child has every right to feel angry, but the child does not automatically have to hit the child who cut in line. The angry child can still choose—to hit, to butt in line in front of the offender, to use words to tell the child to get in line, or to get an adult's help. Help your child learn alternatives to hitting.

Teach your child a simple "I message."

✳ I feel . . . (use the appropriate feeling word)

✳ When you . . . (describe the behavior)

✳ Because . . . (the reason)

✳ I want you to . . . (the behavior the child wants)

In this situation, it might sound like:

✳ I feel angry

✳ When you cut in line for the slide,

✳ Because I have been waiting my turn and it's not fair to butt in line.

✳ I want you to go to the back of the line and your turn.

What a great life lesson and skill to begin to learn at a very young age, although it may take a lifetime to live this consistently. And it is a wonderful tool for parents and all of God's children to use. It is respectful and effective.

DECISIONS

Decisions are divided into the ones that can be made by the child and the ones that parents need to make. How do you decide to whom the decision belongs? Consider the consequences. Will it impact the health or safety of the child? Then the parent makes the decision. Is it an issue of legality or morality? Then the parent makes the decision. What is the impact on others? If it is harmful, the parent decides.

Children can make decisions such as:

* whether they want a friend over to play

* which toy to play with

* not to eat the offered food if they are willing to be hungry before the next meal

* to be tired if they decide not to sleep during naptime

Parents get to decide:

* to give prescribed medicine to the child

* to leave on time for school, work, or an appointment

* when it is time for meals and what will be served

* to hold a child's hand when crossing the street

My children taught me some of the limits of my decision making. I can put a child to bed, but not force him or her to sleep. I can put food in a child's mouth, but not get the child to swallow it. I can take a child to the bathroom, but not always get him or her to use the toilet. There is a better way to handle decisions with children.

BE CLEAR ABOUT WHICH DECISIONS ARE YOURS. Help children know that they can make some decisions, but not all of them. Tell them that you will give them choices when possible.

* Tell your child that this is your decision to make.

* Describe the decision you have made in language the child can understand.

* Don't confuse your child by asking a question, when you aren't really asking for input. (For example don't ask "Do you want to take your bath now?" when you really mean "It's time to get in the tub.")

BE CLEAR AND CONSISTENT ABOUT CONSEQUENCES. Children love to have a consistent, predictable, and reliable world. Consistency breeds security. Inconsistency invites testing by the child. Here are examples of clear logical consequences for behavior.

* If you don't get ready for bed on time, there will be no time to read stories.

* If you fuss at the table, you will get a time out.

* When you clean up your room, then we will go to the park. (Which means if you don't clean up your room, we won't.)

EXPLAIN THE REASONS FOR YOUR DECISION. By explaining your reason, you will help your child build his or her understanding of how the world works and to feel respected by you. This helps your child learn what to expect your decisions will be in similar situations and to learn to make their own decisions.

Children who ask over and over again for the reason are simply keeping you engaged and giving them attention. It's just a delaying tactic.

Explain once. Then, ask your child to repeat the reason. You are checking for understanding. Next time your child asks, refer to what your child said was the reason.

TEACHING DECISION MAKING

Long before you teach this process with your young child, let your child hear you describe the process as you use it to make and evaluate a decision. Then it will already be familiar. If your child doesn't remember, provide an abbreviated version of how you made a recent decision. Remember, modeling is the most powerful of teaching tools.

There are simple steps to use in teaching your child to make a decision, evaluate how it turned out, learn from it, and recover from mistakes. (These are also the steps to solving a problem!)

* Name it and brainstorm the options.

* Consider consequences of each choice.

* Choose and do it.

* Evaluate.

* What did you learn?

Here is an example of a simple decision to be made by a four-year old. Sam has to decide whether or not to go to the birthday party of Reggie, a boy in his nursery school he doesn't know well.

NAME IT AND BRAINSTORM THE OPTIONS. "Sam, you need to decide whether or not to go to Reggie's birthday party on Saturday."

CONSIDER CONSEQUENCES OF EACH CHOICE. "Let's think through the two choices, what you'd like about each, and what would be hard for you. What would you like about going to the party?"

"I'd get to see my other friends and there will probably be games and ice cream."

"What would be hard for you?"

"I don't know Reggie very well and I don't know his mom or his house or whether he has a dog. And I might miss you."

"Sam, if you don't go, what will you like about that?"

"I'd get to be home with you, Mom, and not worry about a dog or his house or anything."

"What would you miss if you don't go to the party, Sam?"

"All my friends might talk about it at school and I will feel left out. Kids might think Reggie doesn't like me and didn't invite me."

> The prescription for learning to choose is to make choices.

CHOOSE AND DO IT. "Sam, are you ready to decide? Is there anything else you need to decide?"

"Mom, I think I'll go, but would you walk me up to the door and stay with me for a little while?"

"Yes, Sam, I'd be happy to do that."

EVALUATE. This is simply a way to sum up and evaluate how the decision worked out. After the party, Mom and Sam talk about it, and Mom helps Sam name how it went.

"Sam, how was the party? What was the best? What was the hardest?"

"Mom, only the walking in was hard, because I was scared. When the party started, I had fun. All of my friends were there and we played and played. Can I have Reggie over to play?"

In this outcome, clearly Sam is happy with his decision.

Let's imagine for a moment that the party had turned out differently. Sam missed his mom, felt left out, and was miserable. Then the conversation might sound something like this:

"Sam, you sound sad and relieved that it is over. You were very brave to try this. I am so sorry that you had a hard time. What do you wish you had decided?"

"Mom, I wish I had stayed home, but I would never have known, if I hadn't tried."

"So Sam, it sounds like it was a hard party for you, but you are glad you tried it. Is that right?"

Ambivalence isn't only for adults! Sam's mom helped Sam sort out the pluses and the minuses.

WHAT DID YOU LEARN? In the first, happy scenario, Sam may have said, "I learned that sometimes when I try something new, it is fun and I am glad I tried. I was brave! I might do that again."

In the second, unhappy scenario, Sam may have said, "I learned I can do it, Mom, but that I won't go to play with Reggie again. When I have friends over, I will be nice to them and share my toys, so they aren't sad."

Either way, Sam learned some important lessons.

IF A DECISION IS A MISTAKE

Know that you can help your child learn from a poor decision, when outcomes didn't work for the child. For all of us, the lessons learned from a mistake are often memorable and help shape the rest of our lives. Mistakes are not character flaws or a fall from grace, but learning opportunities, depending on how a parent helps a child recover from mistakes and learn from them.

Thomas Edison was interviewed by a newspaper reporter on the day after he successfully lit the first incandescent light bulb. "How did you know what to use for the filament?" the reporter queried.

"Actually," Edison replied, "that was the 10,000th filament I tried."

Incredulous, the reporter wondered, "Do you mean to tell me that you had 9,999 failures?"

"No," Edison responded, "I ruled out 9,999 things that didn't work!"

What a different way to frame a mistake—ruling out the things that don't work. How might you help your child recover from a mistake? Here are a few steps.

NAME IT AND OWN IT. Teach your child to say what he or she did wrong and claim responsibility. This is confession.

APOLOGIZE. Ask for and receive forgiveness. "I am so sorry. Can you forgive me?"

MAKE IT RIGHT OR BETTER. Do what you can to make it right or improve it.

LEARN FROM IT. What did you learn? How will you avoid the same mistake again?

MOVE ON. Don't get stuck. Receive grace and move on.

AS CHILDREN GROW OLDER

The older children become, the more freedom they have to make choices and decisions. This is how we equip our children to live in the world without parents to make all of their choices and decisions. This is why we give them lots of experiences making choices and decisions—and allow them to make mistakes—to learn how to deal with those mistakes and recover from them.

Children of all ages need a balance between boundaries that keep them safe and space to explore. They need opportunities to:

- discover their world
- explore their gifts, talents, and preferences, to discover who they are uniquely created to be
- make choices, to help them learn to make good decisions
- fail, experience consequences, and learn to recover from mistakes
- know that they are loved, no matter what

FOUR KEY Family Activities

- ○ Give your child at least two choices every day.

- ○ Let your child overhear you making a decision.

- ○ Walk your child through the process of making a decision or resolving a problem all the way to the evaluation and learning.

- ○ Catch your child making a good choice or decision and affirm the child.

- ○ Help your child recover from a mistake, viewing it as a chance to learn.

- ○ In a bedtime prayer, thank God for giving us freedom to make choices and decisions, for helping us to make good ones, and for forgiving us when we make mistakes.

9

The Way to Treat Others

In everything do to others as you would have them do to you.
Matthew 7:12

THE MESSAGES WE HEAR from our culture are ones
like "Look out for number one" or "The best defense is a good
offense."

But Jesus' messages about how we are to treat others are
the opposite—they are counterintuitive and countercultural.
Jesus didn't hang out with the popular crowd. In fact, he often
befriended those that the "nice people" looked down on. Even
his disciples didn't always approve of or understand why Jesus
invited those who were scorned, marginalized, and despised by
society to be his friends.

These are powerful lessons for children (and their parents)
to hear again and again. Use a children's Bible to read stories
about Jesus relating to others. Ask your child, "Why was Jesus
nice to people to whom others were mean?" "How do you think
it made the person feel to whom Jesus was kind?" "Who might

need you to be a friend?" "How could you do that?" This is a perfect example of how a caring conversation includes scripture and becomes a devotion that will shape the child you love. It also may become a loving act of service, as your child includes and befriends a child that others exclude or ridicule.

Make sure you read stories of Jesus forgiving others, even those who betrayed him and killed him. When your child needs to apologize to another person or to God, remind your child that God is always ready to forgive. To be a baptized child of God is to know that we are loved and forgiven, not loved and perfect.

MODEL CARING BEHAVIOR

Children hear every word you ever say and see everything you ever do. Be intentional about showing your child how you believe others should be treated—the ones you love and the ones you really don't like very much. Tell your child why you are respectful of someone who is not respectful of you. We do it because Jesus first loved us and treats us like friends, even and especially when we are not worthy.

Consider the behaviors that you hope to see in your children, now and in the future. Let them watch you treating others that way. Let them experience you treating them that way. Describe what you are doing and why.

* Use "please" and "thank you" generously with your child and with others.

* Listen attentively when someone is speaking to you.

* Don't interrupt.

* Find the humor in a situation.

* Never laugh at your child or any other person.

* Don't use name-calling or put-downs.

* Keep your tone of voice gentle and respectful.

* Don't yell or scream; don't hit or threaten others.

* Share and take turns.

* Be generous.

* Look for the good and for the image of God in every person you meet.

What are some other behaviors you want to teach your child, as you raise him or her to treat others with the love of Christ?

Of course you are overwhelmed by the list! Not one of us is going to be able to do this all consistently. You will violate every rule you have for how people are to be treated. You will not treat others as you want your children to treat them.

The apostle Paul had the same experience and expressed it in a way every parent can understand: "I do not understand my own actions. For I do not do what I want, but I do the very thing that I hate" (Romans 7:15).

This is a perfect time to understand that you, too, need a Savior who forgives you. And then you have the opportunity to model another vitally important behavior: apologizing.

One of my least favorite behaviors in people of any age is to defend indefensible behavior. "Well, if you hadn't made me so mad, I would never have yelled." "It's not my fault. He was being a jerk." Instead, let's model and teach our kids to say things such as these.

* I am so sorry.

* I should never have (fill in the blank with the behavior you wish you could take back).

* Will you forgive me?

* Instead, I wish I had said (fill in the blank with what you wish you had said).

An explanation sounds too much like an excuse. Just keep it clean. Be apologetic and ask for forgiveness. If you are the one receiving the apology, please say, "I forgive you" not, "Oh, no problem."

Sometimes we arrive at the end of a very challenging day, depleted, exhausted, and disappointed in our children and in ourselves. This is the time to sink to our knees, turn toward God, and say, "Help me, help me, help me." And God, who is already there, already has.

Take a deep breath, accept God's forgiveness, and tiptoe into your child's room. Stand by the crib or bed and fall in love with your child all over again. Let God wipe the defeat and disappointment away, and be prepared to awake with, "This is the day that the Lord has made; let us rejoice and be glad in it" (Psalm 118:24) on your lips. Take your morning shower and remember your baptism. Today, you are washed clean. You are God's new creation. Hear the refrain from Revelation 21:5: "See, I am making all things new." That includes you!

And here are a few other ways to teach your child how to treat others.

* Read books to your child that model the behaviors you want your child to learn or ones that show the consequences of unkind behavior and ways to recover.

* Role-play better behavior with your child. (This is especially effective after another child has been unkind or your child's behavior is not what you want to see.) Take turns being your child and take turns being the other child. You teach your child empathy by literally letting them take on the other person's experience.

* After an occasion of unacceptable behavior, ask your child what he or she was feeling. Help supply feeling words, if needed. Then, make it clear that your child has every right

to those feelings, but your child needs to learn to control his or her actions, and you will help.

✳ Give your child an acceptable way to work out the adrenaline from the emotional experience. Suggest large muscle activities: Run. Dance. Throw foam balls in a laundry basket. Ride a bike. Turn somersaults.

✳ After the emotion has drained out of a difficult situation and your child is calm, spend some time reflecting on what happened. Ask what else your child could have done instead.

✳ Try a little hydrotherapy with the conversation. Pop your child in the bath and when relaxed and calm, have the conversation to evaluate what happened. Ask questions such as: What did you want or need? How did you try to get it? How did that work for you?

Sometimes, you will have the delightful experience of "catching your child doing it right"! Don't wait for the huge accomplishments. Catch them being thoughtful, helpful, caring, and kind—all of those behaviors you most want to see. Tell them what they've done right and how much you appreciate it. Catch other kids doing the same things—and tell them. Then, go tell somebody else. Tell adults. And tell other kids. Remember: What gets attention, gets repeated!

REAL MANNERS ARE GROUNDED IN RESPECT

Real manners are not about which fork you use at a formal dinner. Manners are anchored in treating others with respect and yourself with self-respect. Look at each and every person as a beloved child of God. Real manners are living the qualities you have already identified as the way you want your child to treat others.

Begin with the basics such as "Please," "Thank you," and "I'm sorry." Learning to share is one of the next traits you teach as part of real manners. As children grow older, you will have many opportunities to teach them to chew with their mouths closed, to hold the door, to give up a seat on the bus to a person who is struggling, to wait their turn on the swing, and to wait until others have stopped speaking before they speak. Your child lives with you for a very long time. You will have countless opportunities to teach real manners, both by what you say and by what you do.

SIBLINGS

We only make it four chapters into the Bible when sibling rivalry breaks out. Cain kills his brother Abel. Then Jacob steals his brother Esau's inheritance and their father's blessing. Joseph parades his favorite son status in front of his eleven brothers and almost pays for it with his life.

Your children are not the only siblings who haven't gotten along. But we don't have to simply throw up our hands and assume that this is the way it is and ever more will be.

There are some wonderful lessons to be learned in families about how we resolve conflict and differences and learn to get along. These are life lessons and important to teach in our homes. No single strategy works the first time or every time, and none come with a warranty that siblings will love each other and live at peace. Here are some strategies to try. See what works today for you.

WHY YOU HAVE ANOTHER CHILD. My favorite aunt, a single child herself, turned to her two squabbling daughters, threw up her hands, and wailed, "But we had two children so that you would love each other!" No, have another child so that you have one more child for you to love. Hope and pray that they will love one another eventually. Teach them to live together. Wait and watch. My cousins do love each other now and treat one another really well.

INTRODUCING THE NEW CHILD. No matter how another child arrives, prepare the child you already have for the coming of another child. Tell your child. Don't let your child overhear it when adults are talking. Be realistic about what it will be like. This baby will not immediately be ready to go out and ride bikes or play games. This baby will take time and attention and will sometimes be fussy and frustrating. This baby will also adore an older brother or sister and depend on you to teach many things.

Coach other adults to pay attention to your older child when they come to see the baby. Have little gifts from the baby to the older child. Plan special time with your older child. Listen, even to negative feelings. Let the older child know that his or her feelings are okay, but that it's not okay to hurt the baby.

Expect some regression in behavior such as bathroom accidents, nightmares, baby talk, or wanting to be carried. Right now, it looks like a better deal to be the baby. So, baby your older kid a bit and help him or her find the advantages of being the older one.

SET APPROPRIATE AND CLEAR EXPECTATIONS. If your older child is still too young to be trusted alone around the baby, supervise your child constantly or take one of the children with you when you have to be out of the room. Have a simple rule: "The world out there is mean enough. In our home, we treat each other with kindness." Enforce it, so that children are neither physically nor verbally hurtful. "No hitting with fists or words." "That's not the way we treat one another." Better yet, catch them doing it well and lovingly and say, "Now, that's the way we treat each other!"

SEPARATE THEM IF THEY CAN'T GET ALONG. Don't accuse or blame. Simply say, "I can see that you two can't play together well right now, so you will each be in a different room until the timer goes off. Then, you can try it again."

DON'T COMPARE THEM, EVEN FAVORABLY. Comparison fuels sibling rivalry. Know each of them individually and affirm each of them as a unique child of God, with special gifts and talents. Celebrate those differences.

RECONCILIATION. Teach children to say, "I'm sorry." Help them build a bridge back to one another when they are ready. Read or tell them the stories of Joseph reconciling with his brothers (Genesis 50:15-21).

FRIENDS

All of us wonder and worry: Will my child have good friends? How can I help? What should I do if I don't approve of my child's friends?

How do children learn about friendship? They watch us. They listen. They learn.

Look in the mirror of your friendships. Does your child see you cherishing your friends, making time for them, celebrating their birthdays, building traditions, and including them in your family? Does your child hear you talk about the stories you share, the dreams, the delight? Does your child see your face light up when a friend enters the room?

Let your child know the qualities you value in a friend. Name them—loyalty, respect, listening, sharing, unconditional love, reconciliation and rebuilding trust, time together, shared values, remembering, delight, humor, fun, playfulness, loving me enough to challenge me, comfort, and loving me when I feel unworthy.

Catch your child being a good friend. Affirm the qualities you appreciate and name them. My guess is that they will be many of the qualities you appreciate and value in your friends.

Make room in your life for your child's friends. Welcome and include them. Have them over to play. Get to know the parents of your child's friends. Support one another in parenting these kids.

Get to know your child's friends, especially the ones you really wish your child hadn't befriended. (Now that is counterintuitive, isn't it?) Make sure that you tell these children what your family values. Help them know what the desired behaviors look like, catch them doing it right, and affirm them. Give them boundaries that you enforce. These are the children that you will need to supervise more closely.

> Catch your child being a good friend. Affirm the qualities you appreciate and name them.

But there might be qualities in this child that you don't see. Ask what your child values and appreciates about this friend. See the friend with the eyes of Jesus. Yes, supervise the ones that need it and let them catch your family's values. You may transform the life of another child and discover a love you didn't know you could feel. After all, Jesus let us know that we are all family, and he called us friends!

Occasionally, there will be children that are toxic for your child. They hurt your child physically or emotionally. They model behavior that violates your family values and seem to make it contagious. They aren't good or loyal friends to your child. They manipulate or use your child. This is the time to explain to your child what you see and limit your child's exposure to those children.

Sometimes, wonderful friendships end—the friend moves away or the friendship terminates. What is a parent to do then? Here are some strategies. Use one or more of them.

❄ Listen to your child's sadness, anger, or hurt. If your child seems to be brooding, but doesn't tell you why, give them an opening. "I'll bet you are feeling really sad that Tommy and his family have moved. Will you tell me how that feels?"

❄ Grieve with your child for the friendship that is no longer.

❄ Tell stories about the good times.

❄ Get out pictures of the two children playing together.

❄ If the friendship is still intact, but the other child lives at a physical distance, offer your child the opportunity to call the friend or have an online chat together.

❄ If the other family has a blog, go on occasionally and let your child view the pictures, while you read the blog aloud.

❄ Assure your child that there are other kids who are looking for a new and good friend, too, and that your child has all of the qualities that will make them a great new friend.

Teaching your son or daughter how to treat other people is a long process, done by naming values, modeling the behaviors you hope to see in your child, catching your child doing it, and coaching and role-playing the behaviors your child has left to learn.

Take frequent opportunities to watch your child and reflect on all of the behaviors and values that your child has learned and demonstrates regularly. Tell your child what you see. Thank God. Keep at it.

FOUR KEY Family Activities

○ Brainstorm the three most important things your family values in how they treat other people. Make a list and post it on the refrigerator.

○ Catch your child treating someone with respect and say, "Now, that is what I call good manners! Thanks for being so respectful."

○ Ask your kids what is the hardest thing and best thing about having a sibling. Thank God for siblings and ask God for help with the hard things.

○ Let your child watch you with your close friends as you spend time together.

○ Include friends in your family's life and activities and prayers.

○ Talk about what qualities you and your child look for in a friend. Name the qualities your child demonstrates, those that make someone a good friend.

10

Discipline as Discipling

Children, obey your parents in the Lord, for this is right. "Honor your father and mother" —this is the first commandment with a promise: "so that it may be well with you and you may live long on the earth." And, fathers, do not provoke your children to anger, but bring them up in the discipline and instruction of the Lord. Ephesians 6:1-4

WE'VE ALL HEARD parents screaming, threatening, cajoling, reasoning, begging—and vowed we'd never be like that. And then we had children, children who pushed every last button, embarrassed us in public, frustrated us beyond endurance, and tapped dry our well of patience before breakfast was done.

I'll be honest—discipline was not something I looked forward to in parenting. I just wanted to love my child and delight in our time together. And I wanted my child to adore me. I wanted other parents to wish they could emulate me, other children to wish their parent was as patient, loving, kind, fun, and cool as I was. It didn't happen that way.

A much wiser friend, who also is a mother, routinely reminded her three sons, "I can wait a long time to be appreciated." Raising kids isn't a parental popularity contest. Raising kids to become all that they were created to be is serious business.

The gift of a child is a holy privilege. God entrusts a beloved child to the care of a parent. That means that parents need to be mindful in order to raise a child who is safe, moral, all he or she was created to be, and loved and enjoyed by others, too.

WHAT DISCIPLINE IS

Discipline comes from the same root word as "disciple" and is about teaching and training another person to follow a leader in behavior, in values, in beliefs. Discipline is the way parents and other loving adults shape a child's behavior to keep the child safe and moral, and help the child grow into a person that others can love.

What can we learn from the ultimate discipler, Jesus? He created disciples by:

- ✳ showing them the way to behave (being a role model)

- ✳ telling them what he wanted them to know

- ✳ correcting them when they did it wrong

- ✳ giving them a chance to make it right

- ✳ loving them unconditionally, no matter what

Jesus trained his followers to become disciples. He discipled them. He allowed them to make decisions, some of which were mistakes. Then he taught them how to recover from a mistake. When Jesus was done with them, he entrusted them to carry on without him. We have much to learn from his example.

This chapter will explore a variety of tools that can be employed to discipline a child, remembering that the single greatest asset at a parent's disposal is the love the child feels for the parent. How can we build on that loving relationship to shape the child?

The goal of discipline is to move from the parent controlling the child to the child internalizing the values, attitudes, and behaviors that the parent has worked to instill. Then the child becomes truly self-disciplined. Jesus had to do this, too—make disciples who could continue to share the good news of God's love for all people when Jesus was no longer present.

This is not a quick process; it takes decades of living alongside and loving the child. It involves mistakes and wrong turns. And it results in grown children who reflect the very best we have taught them—and then take it much further. Be prepared to be awed by the person your child becomes. The good news is that we, as parents, get to follow our child's example and become more than we ever expected to be. One of the gifts of parenting is that our children shape us in wonderful ways, far beyond our ability to imagine.

WHAT DISCIPLINE ISN'T

Discipline is not a synonym for harsh punishment. It doesn't mean that you are called to hurt or hit, intimidate, or inspire fear. Too often, parents mistake fear for respect. All parents want to be respected, but fear is not the way to generate respect.

In Baptism, a child is filled with the power of the Holy Spirit. The child lives empowered by and filled with that Spirit. That same strength of spirit and will, so challenging in a preschool child, is the very strength we hope to see in our adolescent and young adult children, as they stand up for what they know is right and ethical, filled with the courage and integrity to follow Jesus.

But how do we live from here to there, with some measure of civility and sanity? Let's explore what choices we have in how we discipline and examine desired outcomes.

PARENTING STYLE

Remember Goldilocks in the three bears' cottage? She sees and samples three bowls of porridge. The first one she declares, "Too hot!" The second, "Too cold!" The third is "Just right!"

Parents, like Goldilocks, have three broadly defined choices in parenting styles of discipline.

AUTHORITARIAN. This style regards the parent as the ultimate authority. Parents who use this style often do so because it is what their parents used or their circle of friends uses. They understand there is a necessary difference between the roles of parent and child, and they want to be clear about it. They also believe it is the right way to parent, and that it will help their children feel secure and clear about the roles.

Parents using this style observe children raised with other parenting styles and feel that the children are wild, mouthy, ill behaved, and grow up in chaos. They use phrases such as, "You will do it because I say so and I'm your parent." No discussion. No reasons or explanations given. The child is not to think, ask, or learn; the child is to comply. Parents feel and sound strong. Children learn that it is useless to fight a parent's authority, at least as long as they are young and rely on their parent. Children may be well behaved, but there is little loving warmth and connection. Love is conditional, based on behavior. Power rests on size and fear. Often, there is corporal punishment, without a plan to transition to any other discipline techniques as the child grows older and bigger.

Fear and pain keep kids compliant at first. Then, there is often confrontation, literally or figuratively running away from the parent's control and presence. But often the child escapes the rule of the parent, only to recreate the role of authoritarian figure in other relationships. The child who continues to be obedient learns to obey any authority figure and can be vulnerable to those voices of authority, which do not have the best interest of the child in mind. Abusive, manipulative, and controlling relationships often result because children have learned to play the part of the compliant one. Diminished sense of self-worth and depression are not uncommon outcomes. It is more challenging for children of authoritarian parents to be both respectful of others and self-respectful, and to create loving relationships that reflect mutual respect.

PERMISSIVE. This style allows the child to do what he or she wants, make up the rules, and call the game. Parents who use this parenting style often do so because they were parented by authoritarian parents and vowed never to do that to their child. They believe that children are inherently good and, left to their own devices, will emerge as all they were created to be.

These parents are committed to not stifling the child's creativity and natural learning. They want to love and be loved by their child and feel that this parenting style builds and maintains a close and loving bond. There are no rules or, at the very least, no enforcement: no bedtime, no schedule, no guidelines for where to use markers and crayons, no rules about where and what and when the child can eat, no limits on pushing, no coaching to share.

Intended to be freeing and loving, the child often feels the parent to be emotionally and cognitively absent. Because there is no parent tending the boundaries or because there are no boundaries, the child often experiences anxiety and unease instead of the joy and freedom the parents intended. Other adults are often judgmental and disapproving about the child's behavior. And other children sometimes withdraw from the child who doesn't appear thoughtful or respectful of others. The world doesn't seem safe or predictable to the child. Sometimes, the child pushes ever harder against the parent to see if, finally, the parent will react and engage. This child goes off to school or social gatherings without any of the social skills to engage other children

> Discipline is the way parents shape a child's behavior to keep the child safe and moral, and help the child grow into a person that others can love.

and adults and is startled to discover that others don't want to be with them. And, sometimes, the parent simply runs out of patience and, inexplicably, explodes.

AUTHORITATIVE. This style is the "just right" parenting style for almost all children and parents. Some of these parents learned this parenting style by example. Some went looking for an intentional departure from the way they had been parented, because they knew first hand the cost of the other two styles.

For all of these parents, their parenting style is deliberate, intentional, and thoughtful. These parents know that the roles of parents and children need to be distinctive. They feel that they have every right to be the parent, to make clear, developmentally appropriate boundaries.

These parents enforce the boundaries they establish, but they explain why. They give the child information that allows the child to learn from rules and experience, and help their child feel safe and secure. They treat the child with love and respect. Rather than teaching the child what to think, they begin the lifelong odyssey of teaching the child how to think. Ownership of decisions is clear: Decisions belong to the parent or they belong to the child or they are negotiable. These parents help the child recover from a mistake and learn that it is not a fall from grace.

AN EXAMPLE TO ILLUSTRATE

The parent of three-year old Jamie comes into the family room, only to discover that the Jamie has "decorated" the painted walls with crayon drawings. How would the three styles of parenting respond?

AUTHORITARIAN. Look at what you did! You ruined our walls. That's it—get to your room and don't come out until I tell you. No going to the park or having a friend over to play today.

PERMISSIVE. What a beautiful drawing. Can you tell me about it? Shall we go to the park now?

AUTHORITATIVE. Jaime, you know that we only use color crayons on paper, not on walls. I am really disappointed that you colored on the walls. I'll get the bucket, rags, and cleaner and I'll teach you how to clean our walls. No, we can't go to the park now. When you've got the walls clean, then we can go.

So, it's your choice. You can make an intentional decision to do it the way that yields the relationship and results you want for your child.

DIFFERING PARENTING STYLES

What happens if parents have different parenting styles? It is painful to watch someone we love (our spouse or partner) treat another someone we love (our child) in a way that concerns us. Do we have to choose sides, and be loyal to one, while being disloyal to the other?

It isn't an easy fix, but creating a shared parenting philosophy and style is a project that happens over time and many conversations. Consider the following.

- ✳ Talk about what it is you dream for the person your child will become. Then explore the ways to help that happen.

- ✳ Discuss the relationship you each hope to have with the child in twenty years. How do you need to treat your child now in order to make that happen?

- ✳ Observe other parents and talk about what you admire and what concerns you.

- ✳ Attend a parenting class or read a book together.

- ✳ Leave short articles lying around.

✳ Talk about your concerns and differences when the children are not around. This will feel more respectful and is less likely to make the other parent defensive.

✳ If you are having trouble talking about it, write a note and say just what you want in a respectful and caring way.

✳ If your child is in physical danger, intervene to keep your child safe.

✳ When you are alone, use an "I message." For example, "I feel concerned when you yell at Ben to get him to obey you, because it makes him afraid, but not cooperative. Instead, I'd love to see you use your gentle, firm voice and clear reasoning to help him understand what you want him to do and why."

✳ Catch the other parent doing good parenting. Name the specific behavior you admire. It's likely to get repeated!

✳ Seek counseling—together if your partner is willing, or for yourself, to learn more strategies to get you past a co-parenting roadblock.

DISCIPLINE SKILLS

Here are some skills to practice.

KEEP RULES SIMPLE AND CLEAR. The younger the child, the fewer the rules. Make sure they are described behaviorally. Ideally, state it positively. For example, "Hands are for gentle touching" instead of "Don't hit." Love your kids enough to give them limits. Encourage the behavior and values you want to see.

AFFIRM POSITIVE BEHAVIOR. Remember, the goal of all behavior is to get attention—positive or negative. If children can't get positive attention, they'll go for negative attention. What gets attention, gets repeated, so make sure you give attention to the behaviors that you want your child to repeat. That means using twice the energy to catch them doing it well. "Owen, thanks for eating over your plate. Look how clean your place at the table is. Nice job." "Emily, what a loving thing it is to share your bear with the baby. Now, that is what I call generous." "Alan, great job picking up your toys. That's a great help to me and I really appreciate it."

MODEL VALUES. If you value sharing, let your child see you share. "Ann and I are going to share this picnic blanket, so we both have a place to sit." Name it. Tell your child that you know how hard it can be to share. "This week I have to share the car with your grandmother. Sometimes, it is really hard for me to share my car. I'd like to have it all to myself, so I could go any time I want to go. But, I love Grandma and want her to be able to get around to see her friends while she is visiting us, too."

TEACH BEHAVIORS. First describe the behavior and then break it into steps. How overwhelming for a child to survey a playroom filled with toys and to be told to clean it up. Start with one thing. "Beth, let's find all of the trucks and cars and put them in this bin. Great, now let's find the books and put them on this shelf. Next, let's put all of the puzzles and puzzle pieces over here." Working alongside the child, you model, coach, encourage, and help the young child stay focused.

REDIRECT. Young children can often be distracted or redirected by removing them or the problem. For example, one of our children, when learning to crawl, made a beeline for a stack of newspapers. Simply moving the pile of newspapers to a shelf the little one couldn't reach was a much easier solution than trying to teach the not-yet-one-year-old to not touch newspapers on the floor or to keep them out of her mouth.

GIVE CHOICES. Instead of mandating what your child must do, give two choices, both of which are okay with you. For example, instead of asking, "What do you want to wear today?" ask, "Would you like to wear your red shorts or your brown shorts today?" Instead of asking, "What do you want for breakfast?" ask, "Would you like cereal or a scrambled egg?"

PICK YOUR ISSUES. This is true of all ages, but never truer than when you have a very young child. Sometimes judiciously ignoring irritating behavior is the most successful approach. Consider these things.

- ❋ How important is it? If it is an issue of safety or morality, it is important. If not, it might be okay to let this one go.

- ❋ Can you get the result? I remember getting Kathryn to try a food she didn't want. I could force it in her mouth, but I couldn't force her to swallow it!

- ❋ Is it developmentally appropriate? Pick out a book on the topic of normal growth and development. Check into what is normal for each age and stage with your child. A mother who commands an eighteen-month-old to stop manipulating her: not yet possible. A parent who demands that the two- year-old share: not yet reliably possible. Or a father who accuses a three-year-old of lying: this concept isn't in place until about age seven.

IDENTIFY NON-NEGOTIABLE ITEMS. All of us need to have our child understand that some requests are not open for negotiation.

- ❋ Make sure that you say it, don't ask it. "We need to leave for school right now," instead of "Do you want to go to nursery school now?" Be clear, first with yourself, then with your child.

＊ When it is non-negotiable, Sarah explains to four-year old Gabriel, "God gave you to me and told me to take care of you. That means keeping you safe and helping you be the best God created you to be." Gabriel was intrigued by the concept that God had entrusted him to his mother's care and that she has a job to do. Gabriel regarded his mom with new respect.

DIVIDE PERSONHOOD FROM BEHAVIOR. Please don't label your child "naughty" or "selfish" or "mean." (Our children become what we tell them they are.) Instead, describe the behavior that you don't like as unworthy of your child. "Pushing that child on the slide was dangerous and unkind. You are a loving a little boy, but pushing is not worthy of you. I know that it is hard to be patient and take turns, so I will help you learn to take turns."

USE NATURAL AND LOGICAL CONSEQUENCES. Sometimes letting natural consequences of a child's behavior take place is the best of learning tools. For example, if your four-year-old doesn't let a friend play with his toys in the sandbox and the friend leaves, declaring, "If you won't share, I'm going home!" the child learns more from the friend's action than from a parent's threat.

Sometimes, the cost of natural consequences is unacceptable, and "logical consequences" are the better choice. An example would be the child who is told to hold a parent's hand, but bolts into the parking lot alone. The consequences are absolutely unacceptable. Here, a logical consequence—related to the misbehavior, but intended to teach and keep the child safe—would be to say, "I can see you aren't yet ready to remember the rule about holding hands in the parking lot. We'll have to get back in the car and go home. We'll try this again next week."

DON'T HIT YOUR CHILD. Yes, I mean spanking. Please, don't hit your child. The groundbreaking research done by Dr. Murray

Strauss, Co-director of the Family Research Laboratory at the University of New Hampshire and renown authority on the deleterious impact of corporal punishment, has uncovered some very important insights.

* Everything you do in discipline up to, but not including, hitting is as effective as adding a spanking.

* Hitting children often negatively impacts the relationship with the parent. There are even studies that link this to elder abuse in our culture.

* Hitting can shift the focus from what the child did wrong to a power play. If the child doesn't cry, the parent loses.

* Spanking often results in the child hitting smaller and younger children or pets.

* Depression in adolescence and adulthood can be linked to spanking.

* Spanking is linked to an increase in relationship violence when the child grows to adulthood.

Not spanking places you in the power seat. It allows you as the parent to say, "People are not for hitting. Your dad and mom don't hit each other and we don't hit you. You may not hit, either, and we'll help you learn things to do instead."

And then, there is God's good gift of confessing what we've done wrong, asking God and the person we have wronged for forgiveness, and accepting the healing absolution offered both by God and by our beloved child.

GIVE A TIME OUT. Time out is a wonderful option for kids and parents alike. A time out—on a chair, a stair, or in a room—helps interrupt the behavior. It invites us to catch our breath, reflect for a moment, and change what was going on. We can return with a new approach and begin again. It also means that the negative behavior isn't getting attention and being inadvertently reinforced. For children, a minute of time out for each year they are old is the rule of thumb. For adults, figure out what you need. Step out, step away. Let your child know that you need a time out. Rather than eroding your child's respect for you, it reinforces it and models it for them.

KNOW TEMPERAMENT

Each child comes with a unique temperament. Some children are intense and spirited, and everything is a big deal. When we identify a boundary, they react by testing and testing again. Some children come to us mellow and chill. We tell them once, and they comply. One child isn't a better model than the other; each comes with gifts and challenges. With the tester, we need to consistently hold the line. With the one who complies on first request, thank God . . . and build their ability to stand up for themselves and what is right. All parenting is tailored to the unique child of God in our lives.

TAKE A BREAK

This 24-hour-a-day job called parenting is arduous and sometimes our cup is just empty. We have nothing to share with our child. We have no resilience. It's time to take a break. Think about what fills you up: a call to a good friend, a book without pictures, a movie not rated G, a walk or workout to burn off some of that accumulated stress. Take the time to fill your cup. This is sabbath, a time apart to let God refill you with what you will need for the road ahead. It's important. Take it.

FOUR KEY Family Activities

○ Make a list of the rules that you will enforce with your child. Post them. Talk about them with your child. Check with print resources and a parenting group to make sure they are realistic.

○ Catch yourself being the parent you want to be. Tell somebody else about it.

○ When you haven't been the parent you want to be, talk to someone who can help you think about what you could have done differently and plan for how to do it differently next time.

○ Make a list of parents and other adults you admire who can support you in being the parent you want to be. Include phone numbers and email addresses. Keep the list handy.

○ Begin each day with a prayer that Jesus will join you today in being the parent you want to be for your child.

○ When things aren't going well, apologize to your child, asking for your child's and God's forgiveness. Accept it!

11

The Daily Grind

Day by day, your mercies, Lord, attend me,
bringing comfort to my anxious soul.
Day by day, I know you will provide me
strength to serve and wisdom to obey;
I will seek your loving will to guide me
o're the paths I struggle day by day.

—from "Day by Day" by Carolina Sandell Berg,
With One Voice: A Lutheran Resource for Worship, #746, © 1995 Augsburg Fortress

SOMETIMES, it is not the crises that drop us to our knees, but the daily challenges that grind us down. This chapter begins with normal growth and development and then addresses some issues that are common to virtually all families of preschoolers.

PRESCHOOL BRAIN DEVELOPMENT

Recent brain research makes it clear that birth to age three is one of two times in all of life (the other one is early adolescence) that brain cells proliferate with wild abundance. This time is followed by a time of natural pruning. The nerve cells that remain are the ones that have been used—that have laid down neural pathways for the rest of life. This is why it is crucial for children to hear language in order to learn language, to see objects and patterns in order to make sense of them, to experience loving and reliable parenting in order to trust that the world is safe and nurturing. Daily experiences matter.

For faith formation, this means that it is crucial to begin to pray with children, read stories of faith together, sing songs of faith, worship together, and wonder about the presence of the Creator. Children need to experience the faith, belonging to both family and a faith community. By learning simple, daily ways to practice the faith, children come to believe in a loving God.

SCHEDULES

Some of us love our schedules, a way to create order out of chaos. Some of us are free spirits and would rather take life as it comes and be spontaneous. Then add a child—one who easily becomes accustomed to a schedule and likes it that way, or who may have no discernable pattern and loves it that way. So, what is the right way to live with a preschooler?

There is no single right way, but a combination of some schedule and some flexibility seems to work for families.

Children rarely come to us programmed with a predictable schedule. And as soon as we discern a pattern in sleeping and waking, eating and contentment, it all changes. Infants' brains do not develop a reliable, predictable pattern until about three months of age. Before that, you can try to create a schedule, but don't be prepared to keep it. Maintain your sense of humor and work on flexibility. It will serve you well—for the next decades!

Eventually children do seem to naturally gravitate toward a schedule. They appreciate predictability in their lives. It makes them feel secure.

After three months of age, observe your child to see if there is a pattern to when your child is hungry or tired. It is lovely to be able to work with natural rhythms, but that may or may not work for the adults in the child's life. If you have a work commitment or an appointment, the child will need to accommodate your schedule. To help children shift their schedules, plan ahead and make gradual changes.

FOOD AND EATING

Before your child arrived, you probably had some very clear ideas of how you were going to handle feeding your child—breast feed or bottle feed, baby food in jars or organic homemade food, scheduled or on demand. Sometimes it goes the way you plan, and sometimes it doesn't. One important thing to remember: Your child needs to be fed regularly, which you will do. However you do it, hold you baby and nurture that sweet psyche, as well as that precious body. God provides for us—body, mind, and spirit. You now have the opportunity to do the same for the child.

Here are a few observations about children and food.

* Just when you have figured out what vegetable your child loves, it now becomes the most loathed food, repulsive to the same child who grinned and ate it yesterday.

* There are some stretches of time when children appear to subsist without ingesting enough calories to support life. If they continue to have energy, play, and not lose weight, they are just fine. If you see a major change in body size or muscle tone, interest or energy, get medical advice.

* Food tastes different to young children than it does to adults. Don't salt or season a young child's food to taste good to you. (That is flirting with hypertension for your child.) Texture can be a major issue for babies and toddlers. Lumpy food may gag your child until the child is older. Keep trying samples of food, knowing that tastes change with time and growth.

* Make food about feeding your child's body. If it becomes a power struggle, your child wins. You can force food into a mouth, but you cannot force the child to swallow.

123

✳ Ask your child to try each food that is served, but don't make it the focus of the meal. When it is clear that the child will eat no more and is being disruptive, excuse the child. Don't serve food again until a planned snack or meal. If the child says, "But I'm hungry!" gently remind the child that he or she chose not to eat at the last meal. "I'll bet you're hungry. You have another chance to eat in a little while, when we have lunch." Be kind, but firm.

There is no single right way, but a combination of some schedule and some flexibility seems to work for families.

✳ Plan every meal to include a food you know your child likes, but don't limit the menu to only those foods. Don't serve two different meals—one for the child and another for the adults. When the child is old enough, have supplies for a simple supplement (peanut butter and jelly sandwich, cheese sticks, or a banana) that the child may fix.

✳ Invite children to help prepare food. This increases the likelihood that they will eat it.

✳ Thank the cook. No complaints from the adults, please. Gratitude is contagious!

✳ Turn off all screens during meals. Focus on one another.

✳ Feed children at intervals when they are likely to be hungry. They come with small tummies that need to be fed frequently. For example, serve dry cereal as a mid-morning snack, fruit and a piece of cheese mid-afternoon.

✳ Studies show that children will eat a balanced diet over the course of a week if they are offered a variety of foods, but no refined sugar. Give it a try. Yes, of course, there will be exceptions, but let them be just that, exceptions.

✳ Young children cannot sit at the table as long as adults. Have children sit with you at the beginning of a meal. Light a candle, remembering that we gather around the

one who said, "I am the light of the world" (John 8:12).
Begin with a table grace. Holding hands keeps little hands
from grabbing the food and makes them feel connected to
the people they love most in the world.

REST AND SLEEPING

Rest and sleep are essential to life, but not all children are
born as good sleepers. Some children fall asleep quite easily
when they are tired. Some resist sleep or become frantic when
exhausted.

Parents can help children learn to sleep and rest, by observing a few simple guidelines.

* After age three months, schedule naps and bedtime at
  approximately the same time each day. There will be
  exceptions, but build a routine.

* Create a simple, repeated ritual for getting ready to go to
  sleep: potty or dry diaper, pajamas on, story to read, time
  to rock or snuggle, a prayer, last kiss, and being tucked
  into bed with a favorite blanket or stuffed animal.

* An hour before bedtime, turn the lights low, keep sounds
  quiet, turn off screens, no wrestling or tumbling or dancing. All the senses are quieted, in readiness for sleep. Use
  a soft voice.

* If a young child stops napping, institute a "quiet time," during which the child has quiet toys to play with, soft music,
  books to peruse, ways to soothe themselves and recharge
  simply by resting, getting ready for the rest of the day.

* For the child who has a hard time falling asleep, provide
  some of the same props as for quiet time, but at bedtime.

* A backrub or massage is a wonderful way to share touch
  and help the child relax.

Before I had children, I thought that babies and young children slept all the time. But what I did learn from my children is that each child has different sleep needs, different patterns of waking and sleeping, and different ways of transitioning from waking to sleeping and back again. I learned to be observant and to learn from trial and error what worked for each child.

TOILET TRAINING

Most child development experts agree that children are not ready physically or psychologically to toilet train before their second birthday. Children master toilet training at many different ages.

There is a way to navigate toilet training so that you do not lose your mind, engage in an unwinnable power struggle, or have to re-carpet the house! Here is the shared wisdom of hundreds of parents.

* There are three distinct elements of toilet training: being able to reliably void urine in the toilet or potty chair, being able to defecate in the toilet or potty chair, and being dry overnight, making it to the bathroom first thing in the morning. The three normally happen in that order. Occasionally, a child will master all three at once.

* Wait until your child is dry for stretches of time.

* See if there is a sign that your child is going to urinate or have a bowel movement. Point out that signal to your child.

* To be ready, buy a potty chair or a child's toilet. Put it in the bathroom. Point out that it is there. Ask the child if he or she wants to try to use it. Announce that you are using the toilet before leaving the house or at bedtime, and let the child come into the bathroom with you. Invite. Don't push, beg, bully, cajole, or offer a prize.

* When your child is successful urinating or defecating in the potty chair or toilet, express your delight, but don't go overboard.

❊ When using the toilet is a regular occurrence, buy pull ups and underwear. Offer pull ups, so that the child can manage toileting alone. Underwear is offered when your child is reliably dry and clean all day and does not need to be begged or bargained with to use the bathroom.

❊ Don't stop using a diaper at night until the child has been dry for a week. Then ask your child if he or she wants to wear underpants to bed. It is not unusual for daytime toilet training and being dry at night to be accomplished years apart.

❊ Stay calm and be very matter of fact. If there is an accident, help your child learn how to clean up. Please do not shame the child or ask "Why did you pee in your pants?" or "Why didn't you use the bathroom?" Your child has no idea.

❊ A deadline, like needing to be toilet trained in order to enter nursery school, can create incredible anxiety for the parent. Instead of panicking or resorting to shaming or bribing, check with other parents to make sure that the rule is enforced, not simply written in the handbook. Often, teachers are willing to have your child wear a pull up. Many children will remain dry during nursery school. Peer pressure may well be your friend. It is often a turning point when your child sees other children using the toilet and wearing underwear.

❊ If your child is five years old and shows no interest in toilet training or seems frustrated and ashamed of not being toilet trained, check with your physician to rule out any medical issue.

❊ Now relax and enjoy the child who can bring you his or her own diaper! Your child will be grown up for a very long time. Find the things you enjoy about this amazing gift of God and focus on them.

127

REGRESSION

Events such as a new baby, turmoil in the family, a parent changing jobs, being on the cusp of a developmental leap, or starting kindergarten are all times to expect regression. What's that?

The child who has independently dressed alone for two years suddenly can't get socks on. Your child who has been toilet trained has an accident or a cluster of them. Baby talk reappears. "I can't do it," the formerly competent toddler whines. With no perceptible trigger, the child melts down and throws a tantrum or simply cannot cope with the smallest frustration. Yikes! What happened? You may never know, or you may only understand when you view life in the rearview mirror.

What now? Here are strategies that help. They preserve the relationship. They help your child feel understood and reassured.

* You have not lost ground. This is a temporary blip. Trust that it will change back.

* Try to keep all harshness and judgment out of your voice. Be kind. Be patient.

* Reassure your child that you know this is a hard time and that you will work through this together.

* Remind your child of a time he or she was able to do it and predict that really soon he or she will be able to do it again.

* Say, "I love you." Period. Not based on performance. This is unconditional love.

* It seems counterintuitive, but give your child what your child seems to need. If your child needs a bottle, give one. If your child needs to be reassured that he or she can be your little baby, let it be for now. If your child needs help getting dressed, give it.

You may never know what precipitated it, but it will disappear with no more warning than you had before it appeared.

You will have supported your child through a very hard passage and let your child know that you will journey with them through everything.

EXPLORATION

Exploration is the work of early childhood. As a parent, your job is to create a safe place for your child to explore the world. Eventually, your child will learn to listen and obey when you say, "No." They won't get into fragile or poisonous or dangerous things. In the meantime, create a safe and creative and interesting place for your child to explore the world and learn about it.

SAFETY

When our first daughter was a baby, we lived in an apartment. She first saw steps at a friend's house when she was nine months old. We left two little ones in the playroom and went to the kitchen for a cup of coffee. The next thing we heard was Alison falling down the entire flight of stairs. She had a little bruise on her left cheek. My heart didn't stop pounding for a week!

Our second child arrived, and when she saw stairs, she climbed up one, down one, practicing for a week. The following week, she went up two, down two. So it went, until Kathryn had mastered the entire flight, with nary a fall.

So it goes. Know your child. Supervise like crazy. Put plugs in all the electrical outlets. Put sharp things out of reach. Same for hot things.

SEXUALITY

You're kidding, right? Preschoolers? Your child was born with gender—"in the image of God he created them; male and female he created them" (Genesis 1:27). Celebrate the maleness or femaleness of your child. Start teaching values from infancy.

From the first loving touch, we say this is the way you deserve to be touched, your needs are okay with me. By giving children anatomically correct words for all their body parts, we say that all they are is precious to God and to us. Model values. Talk about relationships and respect and self-respect.

This is the time to lay the groundwork that will enable you to share your values throughout your child's life. Sexual exploration—checking out anatomical differences—and masturbation are normal and natural. Gentle words and simple guidelines for public behavior work well. "I know it feels good to touch your bottom, but please do that in private, alone in your room." "Your body is yours to take care of, not to show to others." "You have every right to say 'no' when you don't want to be touched."

BOREDOM

Your job is not cruise director. When your child whines or announces, "I'm bored," you don't have to amuse the child. Feeling bored is simply signaling that it is time for a change. With very young children, simply redirect or put other toys within reach. Reassure your child that he or she is very resourceful and can find many things to do. Try to keep judgment out of your voice.

Find alternatives to television or screen time. The American College of Pediatrics asks parents not to let children under age two watch television at all and to limit viewing for older children. Help your child brainstorm alternatives with things he or she enjoys doing—books, coloring, playing outside, building blocks, playing with toys, making a fort. Make a list, illustrated with pictures of your child doing it. Post it.

PRESCRIPTION FOR PARENT RECOVERY

If you have been in the workplace, with intellectual challenges, colleagues, tangible accomplishments, and a paycheck, and you are now trying to adjust to parenting a preschooler, you know that this hardest-job-you'll-ever-love is a major transition.

Of course, you love your child more than life itself. Any semblance of control over your time or body is gone. When asked to recount what you have done all day, you feel both hurt and confused. It has been an intense and demanding relational marathon with so little tangible accomplishment or reward to show for it.

So, how will you recover? Here are some strategies.

- ✳ Know that this is the most important vocation to which God calls you—to raise your child to become all God created your child to be (to nurture faith and trust in God and to love God back by serving others with the love of Christ).

- ✳ You have every right to food, sleep, time off, and help to do this arduous work. With a preschooler, you will never have enough of anything, but please eat, sleep, recreate, connect with friends, and ask for and accept the help you need.

- ✳ Know that the pace and messiness of this time will not go on forever. Embrace realistic standards of cooking, cleaning, entertaining, and all of those other things that used to happen quite easily. They will again.

- ✳ Spend time away so that you get to miss your child! Don't do errands. Do the "grown up" things that fill your cup.

- ✳ After a rugged day, gaze at your sleeping child and fall in love all over again.

- ✳ Find a group of other parents who meet regularly; tell the truth about parenting; and love, support, and pray for you. Make being with them a priority.

131

FOUR KEY Family Activities

○ If you haven't done it yet, now is the time to choose a book on normal growth and development that you will actually read and refer to frequently. If you have one, get it out and use it! Look up the behaviors that are driving you crazy. Understanding that it is normal doesn't change your child's behavior, but it changes your sense of guilt and responsibility. Repeat after me, "This is not my child's permanent mailing address!"

○ What is one thing you have done or are doing well? Look in the mirror and say, "Well done!"

○ What is one thing you could share with other parents to encourage, support, or help them with their parenting challenges?

○ What is one bit of advice or reassurance that you will embrace for yourself and your child?

○ Pray, thanking God aloud for both the challenges and the growth you have seen this day and shared with your child. Thank God for the gift of a child healthy enough to generate dirty laundry and navigate normal growth and development.

12

The Darkest Part

Even though I walk through the darkest valley, I fear no evil; for you are with me; your rod and your staff—they comfort me. Psalm 23:4

AS A PARENT, you would do anything in the world to spare your child the "dark valleys" of life, but they come. One of the extraordinary gifts you can give is to walk through those darkest times with your little one. Your presence brings comfort, hope, and a sense of security. The best gift for both you and your child is to remember that Jesus promised to be with you always. Say it aloud. Pray. Claim that promise that "the peace of God, which surpasses all understanding, will guard your hearts and your minds in Christ Jesus" (Philippians 4:7).

TRANSITIONS

Things change. Some changes are wonderful and desired; some changes are fearful and dreaded. Some are predictable; some are a surprise. All changes necessitate transition. Some of us are temperamentally built to embrace change with zest and hope; some are built to resist change and cling to the familiar.

The transitions that preschool children face—waking up from a nap, parents going to work, leaving the playground, the arrival of a new sibling—seem small by comparison to changes that occur later in life. But transitions are challenging, and children need the presence, support, and guidance of adults to learn to make transitions smoothly, to handle fear and anxiety, and to become confident people, capable of dealing with change.

Let's walk through two common preschool transitions as examples: leaving the park and moving to a new home.

LEAVING THE PARK. It is a beautiful day at the park. Your child is playing with two new friends, but it is time to go home for dinner. You've done this before, with shrieking protests and flailing limbs. What are some strategies to smooth this transition?

* Give a countdown. At fifteen minutes before you need to leave, invite your child to play on two more pieces of equipment before you need to go. At ten minutes, choose one more thing to do. At five minutes, have your child say good-bye to his or her friends.

* When the tears and protest begin, use a firm and kind voice. "It is time to leave now." This is not the time to reason or threaten. Just be firm and clear.

* Empathize. Help name the feelings. "I am so sorry that leaving makes you so sad. You are really disappointed, aren't you?"

* When your child cooperates and leaves with no fuss, catch your child doing it well and affirm the behavior. Remember, what gets attention, gets repeated.

✳ If it was a very difficult leave-taking, talk about it later when your child is calm, and ask what you and your child can do next time to make it go better.

MOVING TO A NEW HOME. Recently, our preschool grandchildren moved. The new house is large, light, and beautiful. The yard is more spacious, with room to run and play. The neighborhood is filled with children their ages, ready to welcome new friends. But it was a challenging transition, nonetheless.

Hayden, at age four and one-half, announced that he was sad to leave his house. Of course, he was—it was the only home he'd known. "I was born here!" he intoned. His family and toys and memories were all there. We all knew that he'd love his new home, but first he had to grieve what he was leaving. Here are some ways to help with this transition.

✳ Be calm and patient.

✳ Listen to and accept the feelings. Don't minimize them. Don't rush to cheer up the child.

✳ Take photos at a child's eye level of the old house and assemble an album.

✳ Let the child talk about what will be missed. (Don't rush to tell about all the things your child will like better in the new home.)

✳ Have the child pack favorite toys or possessions and take them in the car.

✳ Reassure. (You may need to do this over and over again.)

✳ Let your child know you love him or her.

✳ Expect nightmares, interrupted sleep, regression to younger behavior, toileting accidents or bedwetting, insecurity, or misbehavior.

❋ Predict a time that is coming soon when the fear, anxiety, and sadness will be gone.

❋ Take it all to God in prayer.

Try these strategies with other transitions. Choose the ones that work. Come back to others in the future.

CHILDREN ARE FRAGILE

All of us have received a package, marked "Fragile: Handle with Care." We know it is breakable and treat it accordingly. When we receive the gift of our family relationships, they, too, should come with the stamp, "Fragile: Handle with Care." Children are as fragile as anything that comes in a package—and so much more important.

Transitions are challenging, and children need the presence, support, and guidance of adults.

PHYSICALLY. We know that our infants are physically fragile. We support their floppy necks; protect the soft spot in the skull; and know not to shake, jerk, or drop. We protect them from things that are sharp and hot and dangerous. Be on the lookout for our older preschoolers, too. Give them safe boundaries, age appropriate responsibilities, and keep them from speeding to adulthood, damaging those precious bodies.

EMOTIONALLY. As children on the playground, we chanted, "Sticks and stones can break my bones, but words can never hurt me!" Even then, we knew that was wrong. Speak words in love. Refrain from meanness. Listen deeply and take seriously the emotional wounds of our children. In the words of poet e e cummings, "Be of love a little more careful than of everything."

INTELLECTUALLY. Our children come to us naturally curious, filled with wonder and a desire to discover and understand. Support that natural desire and gift to be lifelong learners. Model a continuing passion for learning. Find out how your children learn best, and share that with those who teach them. Support their unique gifts, with opportunities to learn. Catch them learning and affirm it.

SPIRITUALLY. Thank God every day for these cherished children, made in the image of their Creator, entrusted to us to love and nurture for a while. In all that we do, help them see, hear, and experience the love of God we know in Jesus Christ.

DEALING WITH CHILDHOOD FEARS

So many things make young children afraid. Perhaps the very first is separation anxiety, fear inspired by being separated from the people the child loves most in all the world. Sometimes this starts in infancy. Sometimes it happens just before kindergarten begins. It is often linked to a time of burgeoning developmental growth, which might be physical, cognitive, or emotional. Think about the two-year-old, making a staunch declaration of independence by expertly wielding the word, "No!" and pushing away, while clinging to mom or dad.

One of the side effects of a wonderful imagination is fear. Our children create vividly imagined scenarios and then are scared of them. Think about all of the children's books that explore that very theme—*There's a Nightmare in My Closet* and *Where the Wild Things Are*. Read these books together, reassuring your child that, like the parents in the books, you will be present and help them work through their fears.

Listen as your child uses resources to domesticate his or her fears. Bella was three when a babysitter told her there was a wolf under her bed, a ploy to keep her in bed. Bella was terrified and didn't want to play in her room or sleep in her bed. One day, she stunned her mother with this story: "I found a little baby wolf with no teeth. I took really good care of the baby wolf who was scared and couldn't find her mommy. When her mommy came, she was so happy that I took care of her baby, that she told all of the wolves to be nice to me, so now wolves are my friends!"

Fear of the dark is a virtually universal one. Sometimes, it can be handled with a nightlight or a flashlight. It gives kids control over the dark. Taking a sibling or parent or even a pet or stuffed animal along to go downstairs can conquer that fear.

Affirm all of the ways children work to deal with their fears. Your presence and reassurance are powerful in helping allay fears. Let them know that you, too, dealt with fears in your life. Share stories and strategies that helped you.

Shaming, making fun of a child's fear, or throwing a child into a fearful situation is not helpful. Please protect your little one from adults who think that they can toughen them up with that approach.

Remember the words of the psalmist that began this chapter: "Even though I walk through the darkest valley, I fear no evil; for you are with me" (Psalm 23:4). Be that loving presence that casts out fear and brings comfort.

MISBEHAVIOR

The goal of virtually all behavior is to get your attention—yes, positive or negative behavior, positive or negative attention. If a child cannot get positive attention, the child knows just how to get your negative attention!

Since what gets attention, gets repeated, it serves you well as a parent to catch positive behavior and reward it with positive attention. That is, after all, what you want repeated.

If the misbehavior is dangerous, physically or emotionally, you must step in and prevent the danger from happening. Be firm. Don't talk it to death or try to reason at this time. Later, when the emotions have cooled, have that conversation.

Dozens of issues a day come your way; pick your issues carefully. Is it worth your time and energy and attention? If not, here is another possibility: The most challenging response . . . is no response. If the goal is to get attention, this strategy doesn't give the child what the child is looking for in a response.

Sometimes the misbehavior appears as fussiness and whining. That seems to flip an almost universal switch in parents. It is fingernails on the chalkboard time. It would be so easy just to fuss or yell in response. Instead, try a sampling of these.

- ✳ Ask, "What do you need right now?" "How are you trying to get it?" "How is that working for you?"

- ✳ "You must feel really frustrated right now."

- ✳ "I can't understand you when you talk like that."

- ✳ "Whiney Wendy is not welcome here."

- ✳ "Where is (fill in your child's name)?"

If you have said you can't understand the whiney voice, don't respond. Ignore it. You'll have to grit your teeth, but it does work . . . eventually.

But what about when your children are being mean to one another? Here is a list of things that have been effective for parents of preschoolers. Which one will you try?

- ✳ Separate the kids, saying, "I can see that you are not able to get along right now, so you will have to be in two different places until the timer rings."

- ✳ "We have to take care of one another."

- ✳ "The world out there is mean enough. The world in here is going to be kind and safe and loving."

* ✳ "Are you being the person you want to be?"

* ✳ "This is so unlike you." Then, tell a story about a time this child was kind.

* ✳ Trust that they will come back to being their best selves, the people you know them to be.

TRAGEDY AND LOSS FOR CHILDREN

None of us want our children to know loss or pain, suffering, or tragedy. We'd like to insulate them from illness, injury, death, terrorism, and natural disaster. We'd love to preserve their innocence. But that isn't possible.

Tragedies and losses may be international, national, regional, or intensely personal: tsunamis or hurricanes, floods or droughts, wars between nations or civil wars, terrorism, plane crashes, car accidents, school shootings, injustice, life-threatening illness, death of a loved one, end of a relationship, domestic violence, or death of a dream. And, what about the children?

As parents, we have so little control over the losses our children will experience, but we can be present with children in times of loss and sorrow, teaching them how to live in and through the hardest times. What better gift can you give your child than helping him or her learn to handle loss and tragedy? Name it, look it full in the face, grieve it, find hope in God's presence and promises, and move on. But how?

Here is what to avoid.

* ✳ Telling children that it is God's plan. God does not cause death and destruction, but promises to be with us in the midst of loss. God brings hope and a future.

* ✳ Watching televised accounts, hour after hour. Young children, who do not understand replays, assume that the tragedy happens over and over again.

❈ Talking about it obsessively within earshot of children.

❈ Assuming kids won't hear, see, or understand the tragedy.

❈ Denying, diminishing, or demeaning the loss.

❈ Insulating them from the loss.

Here is how to help.

❈ Tell children, simply, in age-appropriate language, what has happened. Let them hear it from you.

❈ Name the loss.

❈ Be present with them.

❈ Listen to them.

❈ Answer their questions honestly. Sometimes, the answer is "I don't know."

❈ Name their feelings and give them permission to feel what they feel.

❈ Grieve together.

❈ Be present in a community of love, hope, and faith. Don't try to do it alone.

❈ Tell and model for them the hope we have in Jesus Christ, who has promised to be with us always, that this life isn't the end of the story.

❈ Pray.

❈ Do service that makes a difference to others.

❈ If you or your child gets "stuck" in grief or reliving the tragedy, please seek good professional help.

FOUR KEY Family Activities

- ○ With a child who has a difficult time with change, affirm that you know how hard it is and offer a few ideas to make it go more smoothly.

- ○ Reassure young children that transitions become easier.

- ○ Pray for and with those in transition. Claim Jesus' presence and power to still the storms of life.

- ○ When your child experiences fear, share a story about a fear you dealt with as a child. Who helped you deal with it? How? Reassure your child that you will be with him or her and that Jesus promised to always be present.

- ○ Read books together about children who have faced the same hard issues.

- ○ When your child misbehaves, ask, "What do you need? What are you doing to get it? How is that working for you?"

- ○ Plan regular one-on-one time together, doing what your child really loves to do, and showering your child with positive attention.

- ○ At dinner, invite each to share one thing in their lives that is challenging, hard, painful, and in need of understanding.

- ○ Tuck your children into bed in the dark. Then, just listen.

- ○ When a tragedy occurs, gather as a family and pray for all affected. Plan one concrete thing that you can do.

- ○ Select or make a special Christmas tree ornament to commemorate a loss, a concern, or a sorrow your family has experienced this year.

13

Defending Your Child

IT'S BEEN a terrible, horrible, no good, very bad day. Your child feels like he or she can't do anything right. Everyone is unfair. No one likes him or her. Your child is deflated and defeated. So, what are you as the parent to do for this, your youngest, most beloved neighbor? With children, what does it mean "to come to their defense, speak well of them, and interpret everything they do in the best possible light"?

Lynn, mother of two preschoolers, puts it succinctly, "Your children are going to misbehave—that is a fact!" *How* you support or guide them through these experiences is very important so that they can learn from the experiences and feel supported. So, what does this look like?

AN EXAMPLE

It is almost time for dinner when the phone rings. An irate caller imperiously demands, "Do you know what your child did on the playground in daycare today? Bit my son, that's what! What kind of a kid are you raising? Don't you teach her anything?"

Dinner is ruined. Your stomach is in the basement. How could this be your child? How could she embarrass you like this? Maybe you'll just change daycares before tomorrow.

This is a hard one—hard for you and hard for your child. You are humiliated and horrified. You are afraid you are raising a monster. What will this child become? How could this have happened? What do you do now?

FIND OUT WHAT HAPPENED. First, take a very deep breath. Maybe two or three. Thank the parent for calling and tell him or her you'll deal with it and call back the following day.

Who can you talk to in order to find out what really happened? Try going early the next morning and ask to speak privately to a teacher or aide, who can help you piece together the whole story.

If your child is verbal, ask your child, "Can you tell me what happened on the playground today?" or "I understand that Bradley got bitten on the playground. Can you tell me about that?"

Children do not have the concept of truth telling or lying until about age seven. As a preschooler, your child may tell you what they really wished had happened.

Until you know what really happened, please don't accuse your child or excuse their behavior.

HELP YOUR CHILD RECOVER FROM A MISTAKE. If you find out that your child did indeed bite another child, find a quiet time with just your child to talk about it. Don't ask her if she bit. Simply tell her that you know she bit Bradley on the playground. Otherwise, it is easy to get into a "trust trap" game, setting your child up to lie to you.

Simply, kindly, and clearly share your values. Hold your child. Use a soft voice: "It is not okay to bite, even if you are frustrated or upset or tired of waiting your turn. People are not for biting. I'm going to help you do three things now."

Pray a simple, non-shaming prayer, asking for God's forgiveness, asking that your daughter and Bradley can become friends again. Ask God to give your daughter the courage to tell Bradley she is sorry and the strength not to do it again. Reassure her that God is ready to forgive us when we ask. Asking for forgiveness helps us to feel better, too.

Parents are life coaches.

Then practice a role play telling Bradley you are sorry. Switch roles. Tell your daughter it takes courage to say, "I am sorry" and that you know she can do it.

Spend a few minutes brainstorming what she can do instead of biting next time. Ask her which one she will use. Don't give her the ideas. If she can't think of any right now, share a way you've seen her deal with frustration in the past. Ask, "What do you think might happen if you ask Ms. Land to help you?" or "What do you suppose would happen if you told Bradley you'd like the next turn?"

Parents are life coaches. We help our children learn to deal with mistakes, avoid them next time, name their feelings, and predict that very soon they'll be the person you know they can be.

UNJUSTLY ACCUSED

Of course you will stand up for your child when someone accuses your child of something he or she didn't do. That needs to extend to authority figures, like teachers, neighbors, family members, and other adults. Your child needs to know that you will back him or her when your child is being wronged. Justice needs to begin in the home. This is the only way a child learns that the world can be just. (Note: This does not mean that you will lie or cover for them or insulate them from the consequences of misbehavior. Help them learn to accept responsibility and make it right when they have done wrong.)

Let your child know that you will speak the truth to another person, even if it's an angry neighbor or grandparent or a teacher. For a very young child, you need to speak up and defend the child.

Alex had just arrived home from a play date when Trevor's mother called, accusing Alex of dumping bins of toys on the floor in Trevor's room. Dan, Alex's dad, talked to him about it, found out Trevor had done it, saying his mom didn't mind. Dan and Alex walked over to Trevor's house and talked with Trevor and his mom. All four cleaned up the play area, and Alex walked home, hand-in-hand with his dad, knowing that his dad would stand up for him.

And don't we all wish it worked out this harmoniously and justly every time? Sometimes it doesn't get resolved or isn't just for our child. A next door neighbor routinely accused Jennifer's daughter Anna of bad language and saying hurtful things to other children. Wise Jennifer checked it out with her daughter and with other adults who were present. Then, she went to talk to her neighbor. She opened with, "I certainly know that Anna is not perfect, but I have checked it out and she did not do the things you and your daughter have accused her of doing and saying." When the other mother did not relent, and in fact, continued to unjustly accuse Anna of bad behavior, Jennifer had to call a halt to allowing the girls to play together. Then, she listened to how sad her daughter was to not to be able to play with the girl next door. We all wish we had a magic wand that we could wave and resolve conflict fairly, keeping relationships intact. That doesn't always happen. Jennifer couldn't fix the problem, but Anna knew that her mother would listen to her, stand up for her, hear her feelings, and not allow the abuse to continue. Let this be the model for all of us.

LABELING THE CHILD

We've all heard it: "My, isn't she spoiled!" "He is awfully shy, isn't he?" "Your daughter is really aggressive!" "Boy, he's over-sensitive!" "What a brat!" If the adult had just punched you in the stomach, it couldn't have hurt you or your child more. What to do now?

Reframe the comment and respond (within earshot of your child).

Shy? "Devon is very observant and thoughtful. Before he jumps into something new, he watches, thinks about it, then enters. We are proud to have such a thoughtful son."

Aggressive? "Ella knows how to stand up for herself and for others. She is assertive, not aggressive. We are very proud of her leadership and clear sense of justice."

Over-sensitive? "David is a caring, empathetic, attuned little boy. His sensitivity is a positive quality, and it is just right."

What a difference it makes for your child to hear their traits as strengths, rather than character flaws.

COACHING CHILDREN TO DEFEND THEMSELVES

You won't always be there to defend your children or reframe labeling. The most powerful thing you can do is teach your children self-defense, which will empower them to stand up for themselves for the rest of their life. This is not a young version of martial arts. This is using words to tell the truth and maintain appropriate boundaries. How do you do that?

Often, this happens after an incident in which the child has been hurt, physically or emotionally. When you and your child are both calm, try the following.

✳ Talk about what happened and listen for your child's feelings, as well as the actions.

✳ Ask what other ways your child might have handled the situation.

✳ If your child doesn't have alternative ways to have handled it, try offering a gentle suggestion, framed with, "What do you suppose would have happened if you had (describe an alternate behavior)?"

✳ Role-play the situation, with several different outcomes, taking turns playing those who were involved in the situation.

✳ If your child needs to apologize and make things better, role-play that.

✳ Pray about it, aloud, together.

✳ Hold your child, reminding him or her of how much both you and God love your child.

CATCH YOUR CHILD DOING IT RIGHT

Jessica stood through the Christmas program at her preschool, poked and tickled by Annie, who was standing next to her. Jessica glared at Annie, tried to move away, and repeatedly balled up her fists. The concert was done, and nothing had happened. Jessica's parents rushed up to tell her how proud they were of her self-control. Every child needs to hear that kind of affirmation.

Catch your child doing things right and well. Use twice as much energy catching your child doing something right, than something wrong. Name it. Affirm it. Tell the child that this is behavior worthy of them! Remember, what gets attention, gets repeated.

SEPARATE BEHAVIOR FROM PERSONHOOD

"She touched my new train," Oliver wailed, as his two-year old sister Jasmine reached for his birthday present.

"Oliver," his grandmother reproved, "You are a selfish little boy! If you can't share at three, what will you be like as a teenager?"

"Mom," Oliver and Jasmine's mom Amanda spoke up. "Oliver is having a hard time sharing his new toy today, but he is a generous boy. When Jasmine had her shots at the doctor, he let her hold his blankie. Now, that's what I call good at sharing!"

If your child has misbehaved, let your child know that he or she can change that behavior, which is not worthy of the person he or she is, and that you will help. Remind your child of a situation was handled right or predict that very soon your child will be able to do so.

This is a child of God who lives with you. Affirm this identity and possibility in all you do as a parent.

LIVING THE LOVE OF GOD

My father's favorite verse in scripture was one he lived by: "He has told you, O mortal, what is good; and what does the Lord require of you but to do justice, and to love kindness, and to walk humbly with your God?" (Micah 6:8).

He was just, he was kind, and he walked humbly with God. What a difference that made to me as a child—and how it shaped me as a parent and grandparent, teacher, and friend. What a role model! I was blessed. Now, it's my turn to pass it on. Won't you join me, defending your children, speaking well of them, and interpreting everything they do in the best possible light?

FOUR KEY Family Activities

- Name your child's qualities and actions in "the kindest way."

- Don't let others negatively label your child. Speak up for your child. Reframe the label.

- Help your child practice a way to stand up for himself or herself.

- Separate behavior from personhood. Tell your child you know he or she can change behavior and you'll help.

- "Catch" your child being just the person you want him or her to be. Name the behavior you like.

- Give each person in your family an "affirmation dinner." During the meal, have each person at the table name a quality they admire in the person being honored. Write them down and frame the list or put it on the fridge.

Epilogue

People were bringing little children to him in order that he might touch them; and the disciples spoke sternly to them. But when Jesus saw this, he was indignant and said to them, "Let the little children come to me; do not stop them; for it is to such as these that the kingdom of God belongs. Truly I tell you, whoever does not receive the kingdom of God as a little child will never enter it." And he took them up in his arms, laid his hands on them, and blessed them.
Mark 10:13-16

"ACHOO!" "BLESS YOU." It is a virtually automatic response for most of us. Unfortunately, this may be the only time we bless one another.

God has something bigger and more pervasive in mind. God spoke to Abraham, and said this: "I will bless you . . . so that you will be a blessing . . . and in you all of the families of the earth shall be blessed" (Genesis 12:2-3). Blessed to be a blessing. This is the way that God will bless your children—first by blessing you, to be a blessing to them, so that all will be blessed by God.

BLESS THE CHILDREN

How and where and with what shall we begin? Begin when you first know you are pregnant or fill out all of the paperwork for an adoption or know you will become a foster family or a blended family. Never stop. Here are some simple ways to bless a child.

- Pray for the child and thank God for the gift of the child in your life.
- Collect children's Bibles or storybooks that help you tell the story of God's love to the child.
- When the child arrives, plan the baptism. Then each year celebrate the child's baptismal birthday as the day God splashed the child with promise and claimed this beloved as God's own.
- Trace the sign of the cross—a daily reminder of baptism—on the forehead to awaken your children, send them off for the day, or tuck them in bed.
- Place your hand on the child's head and say, "God is with you today" or "God goes with you" or "I love you every minute . . . and Jesus does, too."
- Build and fill a faith chest with all of the mementos of faith—the baptism candle, gown, certificate, cards, baby Bible, songs of faith, Bible story books. Keep filling it. Use these mementos to tell the story of faith to the child.

You are the AAA Christian who is nurturing faith in your child. You live that personal, trusted relationship through which the Holy Spirit works to stir up faith in your child. You surround your child with other loving AAA Christians who love, accompany, and are faith formers for your child. What an amazing gift you are to your child and to the other children for whom you are their AAA Christian. God has indeed blessed you to be a blessing!

The end of the Christian Old Testament points to the coming of the Messiah with these words "Lo, I will send you the prophet Elijah . . . He will turn the hearts of parents to their children and the hearts of children to their parents, so that I will not come and strike the land with a curse" (Malachi 4:5-6).

In every generation, God prepares the way for Jesus to come into the lives of children and their parents by turning their hearts to one another. This is not a God who sits on high with a thunderbolt, but one who knows that if hearts are not turned toward one another in love and blessing, the land is already cursed.

Begin each day or end each day or say good-bye with the words of the benediction from Numbers 6:24-26.

The Lord bless you and keep you;
the Lord make his face to shine upon you,
and be gracious to you;
The Lord lift up his countenance upon you,
and give you peace.

You are on a wonderful journey, parenting your preschool child faithfully. You are one of God's best blessings to your child. As your child grows, look for more books in this series for faith formative parenting beyond the preschool years.

May God bless you and your family.

For more information about Marilyn Sharpe Ministries,
contact Marilyn Sharpe:

MarilynSharpeMinistries@comcast.net

(612) 202-8152